"*Thinking Like a Boss* is a must-have manual for anyone who's finally ready to give up their excuses and live out the life they dream of. Kate karate chops every lie that's been holding you back with her grounded, practical tools and real talk so that you feel like you have the peace of mind to finally go for it!"

Cassandra Bodzak, author of the
bestselling book *Eat with Intention*

"*Thinking Like a Boss* speaks to the heartbeat of what holds us back on our journeys to greater fulfillment and success. Kate eloquently moves us through the lies we tell ourselves with concrete strategies and tools to let go of the doubt and the stories that are keeping us stuck. The beautiful and courageous blend of life experiences and professional training Kate shares from her therapy background and her time spent as a business coach makes this book one I will recommend to my clients over and over again."

Amber Lilyestrom, transformational coach, podcast host,
and creator of the Ignite Your Soul Summit

"*Thinking Like a Boss* came into my life at just the right time. Through her timely message, Kate helped me discover the hidden lies that had crept into my heart, and she helped usher me into freedom through tactical exercises for my mindset and refreshing truth about my identity for my soul. To say Kate's message is life-changing would be an understatement—I will be eternally grateful for her boldness in carrying this message into the world and into my life."

Kelsey Chapman, author and podcaster

"No matter what area you're struggling with in life, Kate's mindset principles WORK! I'm living proof of it! In her book,

Thinking Like a Boss, Kate pulls together all her life-changing coaching and clinical expertise into an easy-to-digest format that will change your life and business if you simply apply it. She's vulnerable in her struggles, which helps you see she's a real person but also pushes you to move past the lies (as she has) to achieve the success you've only dreamed of."

Rachel C. Swanson, bestselling author, podcaster, and aspiring-author coach

"*Thinking Like a Boss* is full of approachable and grounded wisdom that will make you feel instantly more empowered. I have wrestled with each and every one of these lies at some point and find that whenever I'm up-leveling they still pop up. Reading her book made me feel like Kate was right there with me, cheering me on and reminding me of what I can do. I know this book will be a timeless manual I will refer back to over and over again."

Kate Snowise, coach and host of the *Here to Thrive* podcast

"This book is a breath of fresh air to help you release stress you didn't even know you were carrying."

Polly Payne, mompreneur and founder of Horacio Printing

THINKING LIKE A
BOSS

THINKING LIKE A
BOSS

Uncover and Overcome the Lies Holding
You Back from Success

KATE CROCCO,

MSW, LCSW

BakerBooks

a division of Baker Publishing Group
Grand Rapids, Michigan

Published by Baker Books
a division of Baker Publishing Group
PO Box 6287, Grand Rapids, MI 49516-6287
www.bakerbooks.com

Printed in the United States of America

Library of Congress Cataloging-in-Publication Data
Names: Crocco, Kate, 1985– author.
Title: Thinking like a boss : uncover and overcome the lies holding you back / Kate
    Crocco, MSW, LCSW.
Description: Grand Rapids, Michigan : Baker Books, a division of Baker Publishing
    Group, 2020. | Includes bibliographical references.
Identifiers: LCCN 2019046538 | ISBN 9780801094767 (cloth)
Subjects: LCSH: Businesswomen. | Leadership in women. | Thought and thinking.
    | Truthfulness and falsehood.
Classification: LCC HF5382.6 .C76 2020 | DDC 658.4/092082—dc23
LC record available at https://lccn.loc.gov/2019046538

Author is represented by WordServe Literary Group. (www.word
serveliterary.com)

20 21 22 23 24 25 26   7 6 5 4 3 2 1

In keeping with biblical principles of
creation stewardship, Baker Publishing Group advocates the responsible
use of our natural resources. As a
member of the Green Press Initia-
tive, our company uses recycled
paper when possible. The text paper
of this book is composed in part of
post-consumer waste.

For my sweet baby girls.

*Annabelle, your life gave me the push
to run toward this book dream.*

*And Charlotte, thank you for giving mama
the extra time to meet her deadline!*

I love you girls with my whole heart.

Contents

Introduction   11

LIE #1   I Need to Have It All Together   23

LIE #2   I'm Not Ready to Start   37

LIE #3   I'm Not Qualified (I'm Not Smart Enough, Young
Enough, or Old Enough to Succeed)   55

LIE #4   I Will Never Have Enough Money   67

LIE #5   Making Money Is Greedy   83

LIE #6   I Need to Say Yes to Every Opportunity that Comes
My Way   101

LIE #7   I Can't Possibly Have a Successful Business *and* Be a
Good Mom   115

LIE #8   I Need My Friends' and Family's Understanding in
Order to Succeed   133

LIE #9   I Don't Have Enough Time   145

LIE #10 It's Already Been Done Before   159

LIE #11 I Am My Business   177

LIE #12 I Am Not Capable of Handling Success   195

Conclusion: Thinking Like a Boss   209

Acknowledgments   213

Notes   217

Introduction

f you had told me even just five years ago I'd be a private practice therapist running a successful coaching business mentoring female entrepreneurs around the globe, writing a book, speaking to groups, mothering two babes under two, all before the age of thirty-five—I would have probably spit my coffee out in disbelief! At the time, I was struggling to figure out how to take the next step in my career. I had big dreams of launching a business, but I felt paralyzed by doubts and fear that I would fail. The thought of even starting a website or social media account felt so foreign to me. I was used to the nine-to-five grind—although not so fulfilling, it felt safe.

I wanted something different for myself, but I had no idea how to make it happen. Would it be possible to earn enough money? And if so, how long would it take to replace my nine-to-five income? What if I left my job, couldn't cover my bills, and ultimately failed at running a business? There were times when the excitement and possibilities kept me up at night—I could imagine my business booming and having the life I dreamed of. But honestly, more often than not, I was wide awake with the fear of failing. Rather than counting sheep, I counted lie after lie about my ability to succeed.

Clearly, reaching the ultimate goal of being my own boss felt nearly impossible. I looked at women who owned businesses and assumed that they had attended business school or had investors backing their idea. They seemed to have the confidence and mindset to step into the CEO role of their own business—something I could hardly dream of. I wanted what those women had, but I didn't know how to make it happen.

I am guessing that since you picked up this book, you may be in a similar place. You have hopes and dreams for your life and career, but the vision you're holding for your future feels out of reach. You dream of growing a business to the place where you can finally take the leap and quit that corporate career, but you wonder, *Do I really have what it takes to sustain a full-time income?* Maybe you dream of scaling your business to six and then seven figures, while creating an empire that employs stay-at-home moms, but you fear you won't have adequate leadership skills to execute a production of this size. Or maybe, like I did, you look around at all of these successful CEOs and wonder, *Do I have what it takes to thrive? Can I grow this business from a small home base to an office with employees even though I never attended business school?* I get it. If I had a nickel for every time I doubted myself, I'd be rich. You're in a place where it's hard to think beyond your to-do list. Anything more brings up a torrent of doubts. *Do I really have what it takes? Is this all really possible for little old me?*

Well, I'm here to tell you it is possible! It is possible for each and every one of us to not only reach our dreams, but overcome the lies that hold us back from thinking and succeeding like a boss. You are fully capable of becoming successful in your business—and in your life—if you can get rid of the negative, fear-based mindset holding you back. Not only have I personally journeyed through limited thinking and come to the other side with a thriving business and personal life, I have also coached thousands of women to overcome the same set of lies that were holding them back. Before becoming a confidence and mindset coach for female entrepreneurs, I practiced psychotherapy as a licensed clinical social worker. For several years I worked in the field of addiction, primarily in disordered eating.

After recovering from a lifelong eating disorder in 2009, I began to research and study the mind—in particular, how to *heal* the mind. This became not only my passion project, but in time, my job: helping women overcome negative thinking and limiting beliefs. If I could heal and move beyond doubts and fears that kept me from the success I so deeply desired, so could others. For many years I studied and practiced a modality called Dialectical Behavior Therapy (DBT), which was developed by Dr. Marsha Linehan.[1] DBT is one of the top treatments for eating disorders, substance use disorders, and other obsessive thought disorders. And as you will see, the mindset work that I do with my clients today targets many of the same behaviors that people with those disorders struggle with—distorted perception and obsessive thinking. Through my own recovery, research, and work in the mental health field, I have created a framework of skills for coaching female entrepreneurs to outcomes that truly work. I practiced this modality as a therapist in one-to-one and group support settings, and it worked. Today, these skills are the very foundation of the work I do with my business-coaching clients. I found that if these skills can work with someone who is clinically struggling, they are bound to work with anyone else.

Here's the thing: it all starts with mindset. A mindset is simply your attitude or way of viewing things. The most common way that people view themselves is in a growth/abundance mindset or a fixed/limited-thinking mindset. You either believe that your knowledge and capability can grow with experience and practice (growth mindset) or you view your skills and traits as fixed, unchanging characteristics that will not grow or improve over time (fixed mindset). What you believe about this is crucial. When we are stuck in a fixed mindset, we limit our potential and hold ourselves back from achieving our highest levels of success.

Mindset shifts don't have to be complicated and messy—with simple steps, change is possible. When we are set free from limiting and broken beliefs, we are empowered to move in the direction of our deeply held dreams and desires. Many women have said to me, "I can't believe how many hours I wasted in the past criticizing myself. My life now feels spacious, and I can replace the time I would have spent in negativity with doing the work to achieve my goals and dreams."

The Lies That Keep You from Success

The hundreds of women I've worked with over the last few years are some of the smartest and savviest women out there. We all struggle with deeply embedded lies, or limiting beliefs, that hold us back from success—but it doesn't have to be this way. Some of the most common blocks that I see in women I coach are fears around speaking up, selling their services/

products, and getting visible on social media; difficulty setting boundaries with customers; fears around what others think of them and struggling to show up authentically; limited thinking around what success could look like for them; and sadly, dozens of other obstacles.

Can you name the lies that keep you from the success you desire? What lies and limiting beliefs are holding you back from accomplishing your business and career goals? Here are some of the most common limiting mindsets I've heard from women trying to pursue their business goals. Circle the ones that you've wrestled with in your own life:

1. I'd really love to mentor other women, but I can't even get my own stuff together. I feel like a complete fraud.
2. I really want to launch this business, but I need to accomplish x, y, and z before I'm ready.
3. I see women who are thriving in business because they have their MBA. I dropped out of school, so there is no way I can experience that kind of success.
4. Everyone with a successful business had someone else backing them financially. I'm in debt as it is and doubt I will ever get myself out of this mess.
5. Will people think I'm greedy when they find out I'm making a decent living in my business? I love what I do, and my business feels like an avenue to create impact. But am I letting people down because I'm not serving for free?
6. I finally have someone interested in my business idea, but something doesn't feel right. If I say no to this opportunity, I may never have the chance again.

7. I'm at the age when I have to decide whether to start a family. I know other women run businesses while mothering, but I don't know if I can really handle both. Something is bound to suffer.

8. If I tell my friends and family I'm quitting my job to start this business, they are going to want to have an intervention. They don't understand how I can possibly make a living as my own boss.

9. My husband is driving me nuts. He wants to spend more time together, but I really just don't have time. I have big business dreams and goals, and I am my business—if I'm not present, how will it actually run and generate income?

10. I have a business idea, but everyone tells me the market is saturated. I look around and everyone else is already doing what I thought was my unique dream.

11. Someone recently asked me what my hobbies were and I drew a blank. Somehow in the swirl of the last few years, I no longer do those things that used to give me life outside of work.

12. I think I may block myself from moving forward. When I find myself getting ahead, I begin experiencing doubts and fears and look for every reason to stay safe and comfortable.

Can you relate to any of these? How many did you circle? Roughly 90 percent of the women I work with have experienced five or more of the above doubts. If any (or all) of these resonate with you—you are *not* alone! I've personally experienced every single one, and if you have too, this doesn't make you damaged or incapable of moving forward. This gives you a story; something to learn and grow through. And growth gives us a solid foundation for *resiliency*—a key part of overcoming lies about our capability and potential.

Resiliency is the ability to overcome obstacles and bounce back. And resiliency is the very trait necessary for growing a successful business. That's right—the difference between women who succeed in business and those who quit is their ability to move beyond limiting beliefs and mentally overcome setbacks. It's not their upbringing, degree, business savviness, IQ, financial stability, or social support. It's how well they can jump back up after being knocked down time after time. Resiliency isn't something you are born with. Just like confidence, it is a muscle that needs to be developed and then nurtured. It takes practice.

Many of the strongest women I know have struggled the most. These women made the decision not to let their circumstances dictate their destiny. The key word here is *decision*. We all have a choice. And I want to applaud you today for making the choice to open this book and begin working on what you see as your limitations.

This is not your average self-help or get-rich-quick book. This is a life and business manual. We will dive deep into the twelve common but destructive lies we tell ourselves. Each one of these limiting beliefs has the potential to derail your path to success—but only if you let it. Once you know how to recognize limiting beliefs and fight back, you can overcome the lies and achieve the success you dream of. I'm here to share intimate stories of how my clients and I overcame and continue to overcome each and every one of the lies we will address in this book. I am going to be real and open with you—and I'm not going to sugarcoat anything. It's not easy, but *it is possible*!

Now I am just your average thirty-something woman. There are thousands of people out there smarter and more well-off than I am. So what enabled me to overcome these lies and achieve success? I practiced confidence. I learned to "fake it until I became it." And I learned to let go of what was out of my control by practicing each of the twelve mindset shifts I'll be sharing with you in the coming chapters.

Setting the Foundation for Your Big Picture Vision

Before we do anything else, I want you to know what it is that you're working toward—a big picture vision. What is your big picture vision for your business? This is one of the most common questions I ask new clients—and it's essential that we start here too. We can't disarm the lies that hold us back if we aren't clear on where we want to go and why. This dream looks different for each of us depending on where we are at in our business careers and in our lives. Maybe you have grown your business to a place of financial freedom, but now you want to expand. Maybe you are in the vision-casting phase of launching—you have the business plan, and now you need to take the first step. Or maybe you are content with how your business is running, but you want to dream *bigger*.

The truth is, it can be hard to discern exactly what this dream is. Too often we bury it under a pile of fears, insecurities, and lies. We convince ourselves that we don't really want it, that we never really wanted it in the first place—and so we lose sight of it altogether.

I want to walk you through a visualization exercise to help uncover your dream and recover the belief that you can, in fact, achieve it. (I know, I know, a visualization exercise—but bear with me!) In order to clearly find, see, and achieve this, you need to go back to the simple belief you had in yourself as a child, before the lies crept in. This exercise, which I call the inner child visualization exercise, is a crucial part of taking the next steps. And it's imperative that we examine where the roots of our limiting thinking began.

Get into a comfortable place. Maybe it's sitting on your couch in your favorite yoga pants with a warm blanket, coffee in your right hand, and a furry friend to your left. Make sure the room is free from noise and distractions. Now think back—all the way back to a time when the idea of failure did not exist for you, when doubting yourself was not a part of your self-talk or mindset.

Imagine yourself as a small child. What did you love? Who did you want to be? Remember those feelings of truly believing you could be whoever or whatever you wanted. Before others told you that you weren't enough. Before others told you that you were too much. And before you believed that you must have it all together. Who were you?

When I visualize myself as a small child, I remember feeling limitless. I close my eyes and envision running through the sprinklers in my little one-piece bathing suit with the warm sun beating down on me, feeling as free as a bird. I believed I could be anything I wanted to be. I was fearless. I wasn't afraid to say what I wanted to say. I embraced who I was, and I certainly didn't second-guess whether I had it all together.

Does any of this resonate?

Ask yourself, *What did I believe about myself early on?*

Today I am going to challenge you to get back to that "inner child mindset." Take a moment and repeat after me:

- I can do anything if I put hard work into it.
- I won't let fear hold me back.
- I will say what I want even if people dislike me.
- My potential is bigger than the obstacles I will face.
- I don't need to have it all together to be a successful business owner.
- I don't need to have it all together to make an impact on others.

Now hold on to this picture. Imprint it on your mind and on your heart. As a little one, you believed you could be anything you wanted to be. Go back to that innocence and firmly grasp on to it with each new chapter. I assure you something will begin to shift.

I would like to linger on the dream a little longer as you ask yourself what it is that you really want. I have a sneaking suspicion that your initial answer only scratches the surface of what you are truly capable of. It feels scary to be vulnerable and to confidently declare what can be possible for your life. I get it—we all feel this at times. Let's try this again. If there were no limitations holding you back, finances, education, season of life, etc., what would this vision hold for you? I know the thought of this can feel terrifying, and you may be asking yourself, *What if I fail?* or even, *What if I actually succeed?* If so, I want you to set aside those questions for now. Just say *this* dream out loud. Actually say it. Then write it down in the space below.

_____

_____

_____

_____

_____

After you complete this exercise, I encourage you to take it a step further and tell someone about your dream. I know you might experience some hesitation and fear. And I know what you're going to say next: "But Kate, I don't have it together enough to make this dream a reality. I'll look and sound like a fool. People will think I'm an imposter. Who am I to say this out loud?" I get it. I've been there, and I still don't feel I have it all together, but with tenacity and a vision anything is possible.

Before we dive into each of the twelve most destructive beliefs that hold you back from accomplishing your dreams, I am going to leave you with one small piece of advice. I am lovingly asking you today to keep moving forward. Even if you don't feel ready. I am going to ask you to quit waiting for that special sign, that first customer, more money in the bank, more clarity, to be more _____ or less _____, more time, and so on.

The longer you wait for the perfect moment or sign, the more anxiety and stress you will experience, and the more unclear you will feel about your decision. Today, I invite you to act in a way that your future self will be proud of. Imagine how good it will feel to wholeheartedly dive into these principles and in six months or a year from now be able to say to yourself, *Thank you—thank you for doing the uncomfortable work because look at where I am today.*

While reading this book, I want you to be open to thinking bigger. I want you to leave your judgment at the door. It's very easy to read a story and say, "I can't do that because my circumstances are different." But I want to say this again: leave your judgment at the door! Each time you catch yourself in a frenzy stating, "But I can't," I invite you to replace it with, "Actually, I can." Begin with an open mind, open to the possibility that anyone (yes, you!) can create a life and business of purpose, passion, and abundance.

LIE #1

I Need to Have It All Together

For much of my life I've felt less than qualified or competent and more like the hot mess express. This was certainly true when I entered graduate school at Columbia University in 2008. First of all, Columbia University? Ummm, who did I think I was? My life felt like a disaster, and the staff and faculty would be sure to find out I didn't have it together enough to be a real student. My relationships were unsteady. I felt alone. I felt no one liked me. I felt I didn't fit in, like an outsider in groups. But the saddest reality was that I felt like I didn't belong in my own body and presence. I couldn't stand myself. I believed I was fat, ugly, dumb, and incapable of success. My mindset was so mired in lies and limited thinking that owning a business or making an impact in this world never even crossed my mind. I didn't believe that there was a purpose for my life. Why would there be?

During this time I was struggling with an eating disorder that had plagued me for years. I'd done a pretty good job of hiding it from everyone in my life. People thought I ate healthy or had food intolerances that kept me from indulging in the things I used to enjoy. One evening in my second semester, though, it became clear I'd no longer be able to hide it. I had just hopped out of the shower in my tiny Upper West Side apartment. I had ten minutes before my boyfriend arrived, and I was rummaging through my closet in a frenzy trying to find something to wear. I looked in the mirror at my diminishing frame and panicked. I couldn't go out looking like this—looking as fat as I did. Today, of course, I can clearly recognize this as distorted thinking—none of these beliefs about myself and my body were grounded in reality. But at that time, there was no convincing me I was wrong. I truly believed it. I'd think to myself, How could he love me looking like this?

When my boyfriend arrived, I was in tears. I told him I couldn't leave—I didn't want anyone to see me. Even greater than my fear of others seeing my "fat" body, there was a much deeper fear: that because I had issues, I was no good to anyone.

I was going to school to be a therapist, but my own life was the furthest from together. *How will I ever be able to help others if I have something wrong with me? Don't all good therapists have it together?* This was my question and something I truly believed. Deep down I felt I wasn't qualified and never would be because I couldn't get my life together. Luckily that day I had the slightest bit of clarity, power, and discernment, which led me to make the right decision: to first confess to my boyfriend everything that was happening, and then to go and get the help I needed. By leaning into my own weakness, claiming it, and agreeing to face it head on, I opened up a small space for healing—and for the possibility of actually achieving my dreams.

My entire life I was a people pleaser. I did everything I could to make others like me, keep them as friends, and make them proud. What held me back from getting help was my fear of disappointing others—whether my parents, my friends, or my professors. Can you relate to this? Do you hide the fact that you don't have it all together because you don't want to let people down, or do you fear that others will view you as weak? Or perhaps you feel like you *shouldn't* be struggling with anything. I wrestled with this one too. I was abundantly blessed with the happiest of childhoods. I would say to myself, *I've had a good life on paper; how can I possibly be unhappy? I should be grateful for the things I've been given.* But you probably know as well as I do that your internal beliefs don't always mirror your external circumstances. There are any number of reasons you might feel inadequate or broken even when your life looks great on the outside—and there is no shame in that.

We Are All Winging It

"I don't think I can do this. If my current and potential clients only knew how much I'm really winging it in this business, I doubt they'd want to work with me." I can't tell you how many times I have heard this phrase from more-than-capable, seasoned, well-educated women who come to me for business coaching. These women, many of whom are therapists, attorneys, business consultants, marketers, photographers, etc., have a picture in their mind of what a professional, successful businesswoman must look like. And no matter how hard they work to move toward what they see as success, it never feels like they've done quite enough. And as these women grow, they continue to raise their own bar of what having it all together looks like.

It's a never-ending cycle. "Once I feel in control of this particular area, I'll be set in my business," they insist. Even as they
gain experience and make progress, they feel as though nothing has changed—the inadequacy and the limiting belief that
they don't have it together enough to succeed persists. "But
Kate, if I could just get to *x*, *y*, or *z* place in my business, I will
feel legit and no longer in a frenzy of winging it."

Do you relate to this—a sense that no matter how hard
you work, you never have things together the way you think
you should? That while you may present a nice façade, you're
actually a total mess behind the scenes? That everyone else
has it together, but you don't—and therefore, your dream for
your business will never truly flourish? Well, guess what? This
feeling is a lie—and a big one. It's the first lie I want to tackle in
this book because it underlies so many others—the sense that
you're not enough will spread and infect every aspect of your
business life if you're not careful. This lie will convince you
that even though you've done everything you can to prepare
to launch your business, you aren't ready to take the first step.
It will have you believing that even though your business is
booming, you don't have what it takes to expand. It may even
softly whisper to you that when times get tough, it's because
you're a failure and you should just give up.

Ladies, if you don't deal with this lie from the get-go, it
will continue to spread, robbing each new accomplishment
of the joy and pride it deserves. You'll find yourself even more
disappointed when you reach that place you once believed
would be your saving grace. Every rung up the ladder will only
remind you of how far you still think you have to go. That's
why we have to crack through this lie right now. I am going
to confidently tell you this today:

- YOU are enough exactly as you are.
- YOU have what it takes to create a life and business of your dreams.
- YOU are already making an impact, whether you believe it or not.
- YOU already have the power within to create the success you dream of.

I want to help you believe that you have what it takes to show up as your best self—that you have it together *enough*, for this moment right now, so you *can feel together* in that next phase. Because the truth is, we don't have to change anything about our circumstances. We just have to change how we view them and how we view ourselves.

The quick and easy answer to achieving more peace around our circumstances is acceptance. And the long and hard answer to achieving more peace about our circumstances is acceptance. Many dislike the word *acceptance* because they take it literally: *I have to agree with this circumstance.* But what acceptance actually means is not approval or agreement, but solely *acknowledgement* of the circumstance.

Let's just say you experience a not-so-ideal situation. Your perspective of this situation is evident—there is nothing you can change about it, thus, you have *accepted* the situation. However, accepting that this event happened to you does not mean that you are in approval or agreement with it: *I do not agree with what happened, but I will choose to shift my thinking around it and move forward. I can acknowledge that I don't have it all together and still shift my mindset around this situation to move myself and my business toward success.* It's essential to

27

understand that the work must be done internally in order to experience fulfillment in any current or future place on your journey. Let's dig into how this can be possible for you. Ready?

Leaning into My Weakness

Going back to that breakdown in my apartment, I knew all of this was no longer about everyone else. This was about me. If I did not help myself, I would be incapable of helping others. Until I acknowledged that I didn't have it all together—and that maybe it was *okay*—I wasn't going to accomplish any of the things I wanted for my life. And so I took what felt to me like a huge step: I began therapy. I was beyond scared. I had no idea what to expect. It felt as though my heart was jumping out of my chest, but I did it anyway. Because the truth is, radical things don't happen unless we are prepared to take big, scary steps.

You Don't Need to Have It All Together

Here's a truth—I don't think we ever completely have it together. I don't know about you, but I am quite skeptical of those who look like they've got every aspect of their life in order. You know, the perfectly posed family pictures on Instagram, the clutter-free, stock-photography-worthy desk and kitchen, posting about their perfect boyfriend, traveling on fancy vacations, yada yada yada, the list goes on. It may sound and look amazing from afar—but my guess is that the reality is much less picture-perfect.

Chances are, your life has felt or currently feels more like a disaster than a magazine-worthy photo spread. Maybe you are wondering how you will ever quit replaying stories in your mind of how that first business failed. Maybe you are wondering how you will ever heal from that breakup and find the strength to keep building the business. Maybe you are wondering how you will ever appear to have it all together in your business when depression is keeping you in bed.

Well, take heart: I believe there is a purpose for your life and for your business. I know right now you may feel like a disaster, lacking direction and clarity, but little by little a vision is being unpacked. And do not let anyone make you believe that success requires that you have it all together. That's right—we are not required to show up perfectly from day one, let alone ever; which means you don't have to expect that of yourself either. If you want to find success in pursuing your business goals, you've got to drop the lie that you need to have it together and lean into the truth that you are acceptable—even amazing—just the way you are. You are enough. Just because that's true doesn't mean it's easy, of course—you know this as well as I do. So let's look at a few tangible, concrete ways you can ditch the lie of having it all together and start living as your best self today.

Build Your Confidence

It's nearly impossible to feel confident when we think we need to have it all together. But the more you grow your confidence, the more you become okay with *not* having it all together. I've been working on my confidence the past eleven years, and it's become easier to accept my faults and imperfections.

So where do you start with confidence building? Ultimately with statements of truth, which we also call affirmations. First, you need to believe that you are good enough in this very moment—even as you continue to refine your life daily.

Consider writing one or more of the following affirmations on notecards and placing them around your home to continually renew your mind:

1. My life has purpose. I was born to _____.
2. My life has meaning, and that thing I was born to do will bring significance to my soul.
3. It's okay if it takes me longer than I expect to achieve my goals.
4. I am enough exactly where I am today, and I have nothing to prove.

Second, you need to be able to turn the focus outward. When we hone in on ourselves, we tend to become overwhelmed by our insecurities, perceived flaws, and fear of failure. But the truth is that this journey isn't about us—it's about finding a bigger purpose for our life. There are people out there waiting to receive our special gifts and talents. When we don't step into our confidence, the world misses out. You have something so very special that someone else doesn't have. Don't keep it to yourself. Think about those past iterations of yourself—the woman who needed someone like you mentoring, leading, or serving her with your current gifts.

Third, make a list of your achievements to visibly remind yourself of how far you've come. Take some time to fill out the space below. If you are having difficulty finding five, I want you to think of what others have said you've achieved and write those down. After completing this exercise, I guarantee you will feel more confident than you did just a few minutes ago.

1. _____
2. _____
3. _____
4. _____
5. _____

Remember, you are qualified and successful exactly where you are with the resources that you already have.

Here is a last little boost of encouragement for you. You need positive self-talk to act as a shield to protect you from lies and negative thought patterns. When the false belief that you need to have it all together threatens to undermine your confidence, try using something like the script below, which I often return to as a mantra. Remind yourself of how far you have come, and celebrate where you currently are.

Where I am in this moment is EXACTLY where I need to be. My level of confidence today is far beyond what it was _____. [Fill in with a time period when you had a big challenge.] *There are women who would kill for the level of confidence that I have in this very moment. I don't have to be perfect in order to make an impact and find success in my business. I am qualified exactly where I am.*

Fake It Till You Become It

Trust me—you aren't the only one who feels she's winging it 24/7. Even the people who I thought had it all together with major successes have reported to me quite the opposite: on the inside, they felt totally unqualified and uncertain. The difference, though, is that they are okay with this reality—they own the fact that they will never truly have it all together.

They know that business is about stepping outside of comfort zones daily, even when they're not feeling prepared. I'm sure you've heard the term "Fake it till you make it." I take this a step further: if you can practice faking it enough, in time, you are destined to *become* it.

When my confidence was at an all-time low in college, I began to practice this concept of "Fake it until you become it." I daydreamed about what my life could look like if I weren't struggling with an eating disorder. I visualized being free from the eating disorder and telling others about my story. I could see myself on a stage speaking to women. I could picture myself in black high heels, dress pants, and a white button-down shirt with my hair pulled back, walking across a stage holding a nifty presentation clicker.

At that time, I believed this was something that could never happen, but I challenged myself to pretend I was already there. I embodied confidence even in the midst of insecurity: I began to stand tall, dress confidently, walk purposefully, and speak more slowly. In time not only did I begin making decisions that the confident, more poised Kate would make, but I also began going for the things that felt way out of reach. And to my surprise, little by little I began to grasp on to those things that once felt impossible. Years later I was introduced to a fascinating TED Talk on this very topic by a woman named Amy Cuddy.[1] She takes it a step further and encourages you to practice walking around a room doing something she calls "power poses." This exercise not only mentally prepares you, but also physically helps you step into that more confident version of yourself.

Take a moment and in the space below write about what your life could look like if you *became* the confident, successful woman you want to be. Where would you be standing, and what would you be wearing? How would you be spending your days, weekends, and evenings? Who would you be hanging out with? How would you be impacting the world? Don't second-guess or say *x, y, z* is too far off; just write what comes to you.

Does this seem unattainable? I promise, it's not. How you perceive your future self *is* 100 percent attainable—in fact, she's already there beneath all of those layers you've been holding on to. And I am going to challenge you to start showing up as her today. Little by little, place yourself in situations that feel out of your comfort zone. Act as if you already are that future self—take on her attitudes, postures, and style, even if only for a single moment each day.

This next exercise is rooted in the theory of systematic desensitization[2]—essentially a behavior modification that introduces new patterns of behavior little by little until we've become desensitized to the thing we were once afraid of. It works in all kinds of situations, but it can be particularly useful to us when we're trying to build our confidence as successful businesswomen. For instance, if fear of public speaking is holding you back, consider how you could apply this concept:

1. Begin with the visualization activity above, closing your eyes and imagining what speaking on stage to an audience of 100 would look and feel like.

2. Speak to yourself in the mirror, practicing a simple three-minute speech (for example, how to make a peanut butter and jelly sandwich).
3. Record your voice and play it back.
4. Record a video and watch it.
5. Find a friend or family member to practice on.
6. Give your three-minute speech at a local meet up.
7. Say yes (even though you feel afraid) to an opportunity to speak at your next community networking event.

Now get creative and find a topic that feels true to you! Several years back I had a client who was given this exercise for homework. She chose to record a video on how to apply moisturizer to her face. At first she experienced some fear and resistance to doing this, but after completing the exercise she said she experienced a newfound level of confidence.

Most likely this will be an ongoing process, depending on the size of the fear and how quickly you want to immerse yourself in it. You're not going to go from panic to being on stage sharing a mic with Oprah overnight. However, this is one of the most effective ways to overcome fears and step out of your comfort zone.

The Power of Letting Go

Without the first act of accepting that I didn't have it all together, I would not be here to share this message. I'll be honest, it felt more than intimidating, and I had no idea how I'd ever be in a place of having it all together. But as I let go of the belief that I had to be perfectly together to take the first step, I finally found the freedom to put one foot in front of the other.

I bet you're wondering how exactly to let go of the belief that you have to have it all together to move forward. Honestly, I kept this exercise for last because although the simplest, it's certainly the hardest. We want tangible steps that we can hold on to and measure over time. Letting go is not that. It's a mind, body, spirit connection that *takes time* to cultivate and grow—and it's a big part of overcoming the lies that hold you back from being the boss you dream of. That said, there are some practices you can engage in today that will move you toward a place of letting go. Here's how I encourage clients to take the first steps:

1. Say what it is you're struggling with out loud. "I feel I don't have it together enough to be successful." Name and identify the fear.
2. Declare out loud: "I've done the best that I can do, and now I let go of the rest."

Afterward I encourage you to take the necessary time and do the work to begin to release this limiting belief. Ladies, releasing and letting go of negative patterns takes TIME! I wish these shifts could happen overnight, but that's just not feasible. After you've walked through these steps, I want to encourage you to walk away feeling satisfied that you have done your part and the outcome is out of your hands. I do this by visualizing handing this situation over and surrendering it to God. Depending on your beliefs, this may be different for you. How do you visualize letting go of these expectations?

If you can begin to cultivate this approach toward your fears and insecurities, things will begin to feel easier and lighter for you. My life is ten times more full in many ways today than it was before starting my businesses—and it could feel much more challenging than it used to. But honestly, I experience more peace and fulfillment because I use these steps daily in my life. I quit trying to control my environment, and there's a freedom that has come with this. In letting go, I no longer carry the weight of the world on my shoulders—believing that I need to have everything perfectly together to realize my dreams.

Having It Together Like a Boss

Before we move on from this limiting belief, I want to reassure you that I still don't have it together. Sure, I've come a long way from where I once was, but I still battle feeling like a hot mess. We *all* do—and we can still experience success despite not having it all together. You don't need to be perfect, it's about accepting that you are fully capable of thinking like a boss *today*. You've taken the reins to change the trajectory of your life. If you had never suffered disappointment, mistakes, or hardship, do you really think you'd be starting or running a business? Every moment of failure has shaped you, and if it weren't for those experiences, would you have had the courage to pursue this path? I highly doubt it.

Often what we see as weakness or a lack of having it all together is the very force that has pushed us ahead. And if we can let go and embrace this truth, we can move ahead in confidence that there is beauty in the imperfection of our journey. We have so much to offer exactly as we are. Don't let the lie that you need to have it all together hold you back from being a confident, successful boss *today*.

LIE #2

I'm Not Ready to Start

er blood was boiling. As I stared at her from across the computer screen, I knew it could be a matter of minutes before she fired me. This was one of those very predictable moments that happens like clockwork during my coaching with clients. And in this instance, it went something like this: "Are you crazy? You're suggesting I launch my business before I actually have a business? No way! How can I possibly begin marketing if I don't have a completed website, an engaged following on social media, services, product offerings, and so on? I'm not ready. I will launch my business once I have everything set up and I feel ready."

In this coaching session I was trying to reinforce the fact that you actually don't need to have everything prepared in order to get started. The actual key to business success is to commit to what it is you want to achieve, get the wheels in motion, and learn as you go. No matter how seasoned my clients are, this is a theme that commonly surfaces during our time together. It's the conversation that breaks down walls. Through practice and deep work myself, I've learned to stay that steady rock for them and not be pulled into panicked behavior and negative mindsets, because I believe they are capable of shifting their thinking. Often after these types of conversations, days will go by before I hear back. I know they are still processing. I have faith that the tough love nudge will be worth it, and they'll begin to believe in their own ability to take the next step. And like clockwork, they come back and say something along the lines of, "I'm not prepared or ready, but I'm going to be brave and do it anyway."

I'm not sure about you, but growing up I was taught by almost everyone I knew that the right way to do something is to fully prepare and then take the next steps. I was taught that preparation must come before bravery. In order to be brave (ready), we're told, *first* we must be prepared. The problem with this is that we end up getting stalled out in the preparation phase—fearful that we're not ready or that we're never going to be ready—and we're paralyzed and unable to actually move forward.

But what if we could shift this paradigm to believe that we can be brave FIRST and then begin the preparations to go further? This is a tough shift for a few reasons. First, the unknown is *really* uncomfortable. And second, society has conditioned us, especially as women, to believe that the "right" way to live is to prepare, get our life in order, and make sure we're ready before we step out boldly. But a shift in this belief is worth it. Going back to my client, she decided to launch her new business even though she wasn't perfectly ready, and guess what happened: she earned more income within two weeks of launching than from all of her past businesses combined.

Why Aren't You Ready?

In your business, you've likely been held back by the belief that you aren't yet ready to take the next step—whether that's setting out on your own, leaving your nine-to-five, adding more employees, expanding to a physical location, etc. You've most likely spent hours daydreaming about what it would be like to feel ready enough to do those things. Maybe you've even come so close to starting and unknowingly self-sabotaged your efforts—finding reasons for why you can't or shouldn't begin. If you're anything like me, you've regretted the opportunities you missed.

Going back to that inner child visualization at the start of the book, consider again who you were before the world told you that you needed to be ready and prepared. Who was that child? I bet that version of you was braver than you've felt in a long time. Ladies, let's get back there again. Forget about the most recent lie you've told yourself and begin harnessing the confidence that you once felt. It's going to take a little work to step into a place of confidence that you don't have in order to feel ready to start, but with time, patience, and consistency, it is possible for you. Yes, YOU. In order to dive into the lie that you need to be fully ready before you begin, I am going to zero in on the most common "sub-lies"—the smaller lies that underpin this big fear of "I'm not ready"—that I hear and have experienced myself.

It Doesn't Feel Aligned

Many women I coach tell me that they can't take the next step because things aren't quite lined up right. They are waiting for a perfect sense of alignment in their life and business before moving forward. However, they also tell me that one of their biggest struggles is deciphering whether they are experiencing a lack of alignment or a fear-based, "not being ready" issue. So in order to dive into this, let's first define what exactly alignment is.

My working definition of alignment is when something feels crafted with integrity, within your value system, and has a little piece of your soul infused in it. It's that circumstance that leaves you feeling completely at peace. And here's what misalignment feels like: anxiety, restlessness, shame, the incessant nagging feeling that you might be betraying yourself. You know, *my integrity feels robbed and I want to run and hide* kind of feeling? So, you may ask, how do you determine whether it's fear or a lack of alignment holding you back from being ready? You've got to do two things: check your gut and check the evidence.

Check Your Gut

Let's begin with an example: You've been open to speaking engagements as you desire to get more comfortable with teaching in front of crowds. You are offered the opportunity to speak at a particular event, but for some reason it feels really off to you. You can't quite put your finger on it. You start beating yourself up. And then you begin telling yourself it's because you just aren't ready, although you begin to sense that it's really not aligned.

Nine times out of ten, when you have an inkling that something is out of alignment, it usually is. And if you begin to recognize this and trust your intuition, in time you will begin to gain discernment. This happened to me during the launch of my *Thinking Like a Boss* podcast. I had numerous emails from people pitching to be on the show, and in this instance, one from a publicist of someone I quite honestly viewed as being ten steps ahead of my success. I questioned whether I was being too selective, but this particular pitch really felt off. The woman seemed very nice, and I had no specific reason not to collaborate, but something in my soul felt unsettled. I asked myself, *Am I just nervous to interview her because I feel intimidated, or is it being revealed to me that it's not in my best interest to promote her because of an integrity issue?*

Now I am not here to judge anyone. I will be the first to admit that I make my fair share of mistakes. I have accidentally left the store with something unpaid in my grocery cart and neglected to go back and remedy the situation. Sometimes I swear when I drop things. And I admit that I have hidden and pretended I wasn't home when a relative was at the door—on more than one occasion. But with this woman, I had a sense that I needed to protect my tribe from her influence.

I kindly declined having her on the podcast. Two weeks later, a trusted friend confided in me about a recent business interaction that had gone badly. She didn't tell me this to gossip but because she was truly hurt and felt taken advantage of. She needed a fresh perspective. Though she didn't mention the woman's name, I felt in my spirit this might have been the woman I kindly declined for the podcast. And later, this inclination was confirmed. In this instance, I had used discernment to protect my personal integrity when I felt an opportunity be out of alignment with my values.

That said, it's important to recognize that alignment doesn't always feel good. Listening to your intuition will at times feel awkward. Even though you may feel a sense of peace, you may wonder if others will question your decision, which can leave you feeling uneasy. Maintaining your integrity may even be unpopular, leaving you feeling like the odd one out, but ultimately it solidifies confidence and consistency—and an ability to listen to yourself as you weigh decisions. Although turning down what seemed at first like a great opportunity felt uncomfortable, I was able to walk away from that particular situation with a sense of peace that I had done the right thing.

> **TIP:** When others ask you to collaborate or promote their business, movement, or cause, make sure that what they say and do is in alignment for you. Your tribe puts great trust in your opinion. This is why I will never market a product or service unless it is something that I voluntarily purchased and can wholeheartedly vouch for. I also will not give a letter of recommendation unless I have worked with someone in a close capacity for at least six months. Sorry, three months just isn't cutting it for me! Do you know your limits in terms of promoting others?

Check the Evidence

When I have enough evidence before me to lay out all the facts, I use a simple decision-making tool, inspired by Dr. Linehan's Dialectical Behavior Therapy (DBT),[1] to weigh the pros and cons of the opportunity. Unlike the pros and cons lists that you typically see, the one I've used for years with my therapy clients examines not only the pros and cons of doing the thing but also the pros and cons of *not* doing the thing. I know it sounds repetitive, but when you have a more robust list of pros and cons, your best decision appears much clearer on the page. This type of list picks up more than just the facts; it also picks up the emotions associated with the facts. The

Check out this example!

Decision you need to make: Hire a business coach

Pros of doing it	Cons of doing it
• Will help me get clear on direction	• MONEY!
• She has raving reviews	• I know it WON'T work unless I believe in myself
• I will have someone to push me past my fears while supporting me	• I really have to step up my game and put what she suggests into action
• I know I'll make the investment back	
• At least I know I won't still be stuck in this same place in another three months	

Pros of not doing it	Cons of not doing it
• Ugh! I don't think there is anything good about not having a coach/mentor	• I'll be exactly where I am now in three months. I know I need someone to hold me accountable
• Maybe not putting $$ on my credit card, but that also means I might be stuck in this same spot of not making money	• I'll feel defeated, self-esteem even lower because I'm not seeing momentum
	• I'll be even more broke because no clients = no cash

Decision you need to make: _____

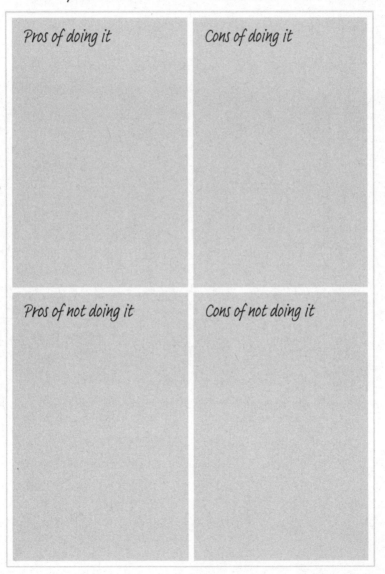

Pros of doing it	*Cons of doing it*
Pros of not doing it	*Cons of not doing it*

only way to fully understand what the heck I am saying is to try it! I've included a sample list that I've filled out, along with a blank one for you to complete.

Once My Circumstances Change, Then I'll Be Ready

Another aspect of the "not ready" lie that I hear almost on a daily basis is some version of this: "I'll be ready when my circumstances change." Many of us believe that in order to be ready, our circumstances and environment must be in a very specific place.

- Once I can save up for the sound equipment, I will feel ready to start my podcast.
- Once my branding is done, I'll be ready to share my website with potential customers.
- Once I have $20,000 in savings, I will feel ready to have a baby.
- Once I lose those last five pounds, I'll be camera ready.
- Once I finish grad school, I'll feel legit enough to start writing my book.

I'm sure you've said these kinds of statements before. I want you to pause for five minutes and take an inventory of your vocabulary. Maybe text a few people in your life and ask them if they have noticed you saying, "Once I have _____, then I'll be ready to _____." Call yourself out. Ask friends to call you out. The only way to ditch this mindset is to first get honest with the beliefs you're carrying. Fill in the blanks below.

1. Once I have _____, then I'll be ready to
   _____.

2. Once I have _____, then I'll be ready to
   _____.

3. Once I have _____, then I'll be ready to
   _____.

4. Once I have _____, then I'll be ready to
   _____.

5. Once I have _____, then I'll be ready to
   _____.

Are you surprised with the statements that you uncovered? Be honest with yourself. Have these mindsets helped propel you forward, or have they held you back? Once you become cognizant of these beliefs, stop yourself, and replace them with, "I will never feel ready enough to start, but if I have this opportunity, it means that I AM ready to start."

Want to know a simple but impactful strategy I've learned from mentors and highly successful people? They don't wait until their environment and circumstances are ideal. They are resourceful and begin with whatever is at their fingertips— whether it's a less-than-ideal workspace, limited quiet time, or crappy equipment—they just get started.

I've had the vision for this book on my heart since July 2017. I had the mental snapshot of what I wanted to include and felt a burning desire to get it into the world ASAP. At the time I was three months postpartum, a ball of nerves, fears, regrets—you name it, I felt it. Anyone from the outside looking in at my life would have told me I was a nutjob even thinking about tackling a book, but I felt a strong tug at my heart to do it—even though the circumstances weren't ideal and I felt nowhere near prepared, qualified, or ready.

Later that week I received an email from a writer launching a "book-birthing program," which was a course to coach authors who were starting out on their writing journey. Having just birthed my own baby, this felt like sweet synchronicity, so I reached out to inquire. The program would begin in just four short weeks, and the odds of making this happen were slim to none. We were still on the daycare wait list, and my daughter Annabelle was not yet taking a bottle, I couldn't keep up my milk supply (which made for an unhappy, zero-nap baby), and the little bit of time I did have, I needed to pour into my business to be able to pay my team.

As you can imagine, it felt like a long shot. Even after completing my own decision-making worksheet and with my current circumstances pointing to a big fat NO, the potential long-term reward led me to a green light. So despite the fear of not feeling ready and uncertain about how I could commit to weekly coaching calls, teaching modules, and finding space to write (with a *clear* mind), I opened up my email and replied with a big fat YES. My anthem in life has always been to say yes now and figure it out later if it's something I want but don't feel ready for.

- That opportunity to collaborate on a project with a colleague that you want to say yes to but don't feel quite ready for? Say yes and figure it out later.
- That speaking engagement at your local networking group that you don't feel ready for? Say yes and figure it out later.

47

- That opportunity to attend a once-in-a-lifetime event where you'll be surrounded by big leaders in your industry that you really don't feel ready for? Say yes and figure it out the week before.

I'm not joking. Everything that scares me I figure out the week before.

Here's the easy, breezy formula I use to prepare for what I feel called to commit to:

1. Say YES to said event or opportunity that you want but you don't feel ready for.
2. Tell yourself you aren't actually scared, you are EXCITED that this opportunity was presented to you.
3. Practice gratitude and thankfulness that this opportunity has come your way.
4. Pray for, meditate on, and/or visualize strength, peace, and readiness.
5. Accept that the only way to feel ready is to actually go and do the thing. It is not preparation that prepares you but ACTION.
6. When your nerves begin to act up, tell yourself, *I can worry about this tomorrow*. Then tomorrow postpone those worries to the next day, and so on.
7. Finally, be okay with not preparing *too* far in advance. Set aside adequate time to start preparing, and also leave room a few days prior for anything that may come up at the last minute. Add margin to your schedule and set yourself up to feel supported by it.

Now this is a very simple process, and I will say that with larger opportunities, you will need to begin preparations much further in advance. Also, I only use this approach once I have explored and confirmed that the opportunity is aligned. Now for those of you who aren't quite sure if you should take the steps to say yes, here is a simple question that I heard years ago from one of my mentors: "Is this a *no*, a *go*, or a *slow*?"

Ask yourself that question out loud, then take some time to think it over. Is it aligned? Once you have clarity on which it is, proceed accordingly. If it's a *slow*, don't push it—you can wait until it's a go. If it's a *no*, that's your answer. And when it's a *go*, then just go for it! When it came to the book-birthing program, I knew it was a go—so I committed despite my circumstances, and because I committed, my confidence in the outcome began to increase. Again, it's about committing up front, trusting that what is meant for you will indeed come to you. Within two weeks of my yes, Annabelle began taking a bottle, eating solid food, and sleeping longer periods of time, and a day opened at the daycare center. I began seeing the light at the end of the tunnel. I would finally have one day per week to begin writing my book. Again, the climate of my circumstances still was not ideal to devote to becoming a *New York Times* bestselling author (speaking this into existence, ladies!), it took work and sacrifice. But the passion in my soul to make this happen was strong, and I was willing to use what was already in my hands to move me forward.

I Will Feel More Ready Tomorrow

When we're afraid of moving forward with a big dream, we often tell ourselves that we just need more time, and that when we feel more ready, we'll do it. But what does "feeling more ready" even mean? Quite honestly, I don't think anyone has cracked the code of feeling ready. The ability to move forward anyway is what separates the dreamer who continually dreams from the doer who gets stuff done! Just this morning a client declared she would no longer be attending a particular monthly networking event. She reported that each month she attends, the same people show up with the same problems, goals, and minimal movement. Do you ever find yourself in circles like these? If so, I've got advice for you: RUN. Stagnation is a silent killer, and like a weed, it spreads. You are the average of the circle you run with; make sure your tribe is moving and even sprinting ahead of you.

Do you identify with this? If you paused and looked back on your life, would you see a movie reel of yourself talking about the things you still say you'll begin tomorrow? Can you honestly say that in days, weeks, or months you will actually feel more prepared? I highly doubt it. TODAY is the most ready you will ever be. Which leads to some readiness pointers I want to share with you:

1. Begin by telling yourself, *Today is the most ready I will ever be*. The moment you set your heart on a goal, begin acting on it. Take small, imperfect action to get the momentum going. The longer you wait and think about the goal, the harder it is to make it happen. And the longer you wait, the easier it is to talk yourself out of it. The more time elapses, the greater your risk of throwing roadblocks and excuses in the way. *Maybe I won't have enough time. Maybe I'm not equipped. Maybe it will just be one big waste of my time . . .*

2. Embarrass yourself. When I knew I wanted to write a book but was scared out of my mind, I began to say the goal out loud to myself, then to my husband, then to my business coach, then to my friends, and so on. Six months into writing, I was enjoying casual conversation over tacos, chips, and guacamole with a group of other entrepreneurs. My business bestie casually asked me in front of everyone how the proposal was going, and I just about spit out my drink and fell off my stool. I turned beet red and started nervously shoving more chips in my mouth as a slew of eager questions started pouring out from the women around the table. They were ecstatic for me and wanted to cheer me on, but I reverted back to my fifth-grade self when I got my period for the first time on the It's a Small World ride at Disney World. True story, ladies! Up until that day I hadn't said, "I want to be a published author," out loud enough. Because I was already beet red, I openly admitted that talking about it made me feel really uncomfortable, and I was grateful that I had the opportunity to embarrass myself. It meant that I was moving in the direction of my dreams *before* I felt 100 percent ready.

3. Write it down. I can't stress enough the importance of writing down our goals, for two reasons: First, we can say our dream out loud, but there is power in the physical act of putting our dreams on paper. When we write down our priorities, they are more tangible, and in turn, they actually become priorities. And when something is a priority, we are more willing to hold ourselves accountable and take the necessary steps to get there. Second, there is something so special about

finding a documented goal and having the ability to remind ourselves of how far we have come. I often encourage my clients to take a peek back into their journal from several seasons prior to see what goals they were working toward. Nine times out of ten, they've accomplished those goals and then some. Seeing the progress firsthand gives a huge boost of confidence. It feels like yesterday when I wrote down my goal of opening a brick-and-mortar therapy practice. Today, as I look back at that journal entry, I feel great pride and accomplishment. I am proud of the grit and sacrifice that went into making that goal a reality.

What is something you want but haven't felt ready for? Can you write it down and begin taking steps toward it today? Take a moment and write it down here.

_____

_____

_____

_____

_____

How Badly Do You Want It?

Two questions you'll see repeated throughout this book are

1. *How badly do you want to reach your goals?* When you want it badly enough, you will do whatever it takes to see it manifest.

2. *What are you willing to give up in order to take steps toward your dreams?*

I know this can be difficult to hear, but if you aren't willing to lay aside the need to have things a certain way in order to get started, then you really don't want it badly enough. I equate this to physical hunger. You know, when you say you're starving and there's nothing to eat in the house even though there are frozen dinners in the freezer and Ritz crackers in the cupboard? Yet you don't want to eat them, and you'd rather wait until your evening dinner plans. Ladies, I hate to break it to you, but we have no idea what true starvation feels like. If you were actually starving, you would eat the darn Ritz crackers and anything you could find to fill your belly.

Same thing goes for your passion. If you want it badly enough, you will take the leftovers, the crumbs, whatever you can get in order to fill that desire in your heart. You won't wait until the temperature in the room is comfortable. You will declare that today is *your time* and your *best day* to begin. Life is too short to wait for that perfect moment to unfold— you have work to do *today*. Begin to look at the lives you may be missing out on touching, the opportunities you may be losing, and the blessings you are potentially blocking. I don't know about you, but I feel a responsibility on this earth to take action—there is someone out there today who needs what I have to offer in this very moment. Whether I feel ready or not, there are needs waiting to be met. In those moments that you don't feel ready, remember you have a purpose to fulfill. How many individuals could you be impacting with bold and brave action? Who needs your very message today? I know for sure if I waited until I was ready, this book would still be sitting in my mind. What gift do you possess that can no longer go unseen or unheard? Like that inner child visualization we talked about earlier, take the next steps for her. *First* be brave and *then* go and figure it out.

LIE #3

I'm Not Qualified
(I'm Not Smart Enough, Young Enough, or Old Enough to Succeed)

Private practice? You? But you're not even thirty years old yet. No offense, but how do you know how to run a business? Most stay in the nonprofit world for twenty-plus years before going off on their own. You've barely lived as long as people work before opening their practice. Will people even trust you since you look so young? How are you going to pay the bills? Thank goodness you're married in case this doesn't work out. Does your husband even approve?"

Okay, so no one ever said all of the above in one conversation. But throughout my transition from nonprofit to private practice, this is the collection of what I've heard. Most comments were thrown in with some kind words, but when you gather this smattering of statements and questions, they add up to one big smack in the face.

Ladies, chances are that if you're in business and haven't heard some version of these comments already, you will. It's natural when setting out to make your dream a reality that you'll come up against a whole host of reasons why you're not qualified. And the comments mentioned above don't even take into account the loudest one of all: the voice coming from within. The words of discouragement I heard from those around me as I prepared to launch my business only added fuel to the fire of lies I had been telling myself already:

- You aren't smart enough.
- You don't have enough time in the field.
- You sound like a child and look like a high schooler.
- You've never owned a business—what makes you think you can start now?
- You're too young and don't have enough life knowledge or street cred.

Already struggling with the above lies and tacking on skepticism from others? I was pretty much shaking in my boots with insecurity. Have you ever felt this way? Maybe you are feeling it today. Maybe you are feeling too old or lacking the education to be successful at pursuing your dream. Or maybe you've had a business for a few years that has been extremely successful and you recently decided that it's time you hire employees— but because you are twenty-eight years old, you don't feel ready to be hiring and training people who are twenty years older. You wonder, *What will they think of me? Will they feel weird taking orders from someone younger than them? Will they question my authority?*

Regardless of your specific situation, I can assure you that the lie of not feeling qualified affects *all* women. Whether we're young or old, with a business degree or a GED, we all buy into the idea that we aren't enough to actually *do* this thing. It's very rare that anyone feels they are in the exact right space with the perfect qualifications to be the boss they envision.

Ultimately, the belief that we're unqualified boils down to one thing: the fear of failing. *I'm too old, so I'll most likely fail. I'm too young, so I'll most likely fail. I'm not smart enough, so I'll most likely fail.* When we find ourselves living in a state of fear, believing we're too much or not enough, we tend to avoid our deepest desires or longings. We let excuses hold us back from taking risks and running toward our dreams. And we avoid opportunities because it feels risky going after something that we really want. But remember, it's so worth it! Imagine how different your life could look if you ran toward the fear and faced it each and every time.

Let's take a closer look at the kinds of lies (or excuses) we buy into about our qualifications—and how we can uproot those fear-based mindsets in order to find tangible success.

Not Enough and Too Much at the Exact Same Time

Sadly, we are *all* hit with the "not enoughs" and "too muches" every day—in every arena of life. Take dating. I remember being paralyzed at times sitting by my phone wondering, do I call or do I wait? Do I text back right away, or will that make me appear like I'm *too much*? Do I wait a day, or will he think I'm *not enough* of a communicator? It's brutal!

In business, we often allow what we learned from dating to spill into our approach to life and business. We've watched movies and read books about the girl who sat around for days or weeks waiting for the boy to call because she didn't want to appear to be "too much" or needy. Are you allowing this societal depiction of how "good girls" should be to take hold of how you approach business today? It's a common way women tend to self-sabotage in business; we fear how we will be perceived, and in turn, we fail to show up unapologetically.

All I can offer to you today is that no matter what, you will *always* be too much for someone and not enough for someone else. You simply can't please everyone—so we've got to learn to be our own advocates. My whole life I've been told I'm too much for people. It used to make me shrink down, acting smaller. But over time I realized that my "too much" personality actually helped me achieve my goals. I'm not afraid of asking for things. If I had continued to hide and shrink, I would never have achieved the steps that are leading me to my ultimate calling.

As we continue to sort through these limiting beliefs, consider the following questions:

- What have people said about your personality?
- Have they said you are too much or not enough?
- How have you allowed being too much or not enough to hold you back in your life and business?
- How have you allowed being too much or not enough to propel you forward in your life and business?

As you reflect on the ways being yourself has in fact propelled you forward and allowed for success, remember that if you try to please everyone, you will please no one. In order to *be* the boss you are capable of being, you just need to show up unapologetically as yourself. You don't need anyone else's approval to succeed. The only way those opinions can undermine your success is if you let criticisms turn into limiting beliefs. You have the personality traits and temperament necessary to fulfill your purpose in life, and as you show up as yourself, you'll attract that tribe that needs you. You don't have to change; you can accept and celebrate the person that you already are!

Too Young or Too Old

"But Kate, they are never going to take me seriously, I sound so young." Flash back to my early coaching days. One of the first clients I worked with struggled with the lie that she was too young to be seen as an expert in her field. She felt that because her voice sounded high pitched, others would not take her seriously. "But Kate, once they get on the phone with me they're going to know, and then they are going to think I am too young to effectively do my job." Through digging deeper with this client, we uncovered that this limited thinking was blocking her from working with lovely potential clients. Whenever she got on the phone with a potential client, she tensed up, assuming the person wouldn't want to work with her, and she appeared insecure as she stumbled over her words. It wasn't that other people were right in saying she was too young, it was *her own* belief about being too young that was ultimately holding her back.

You are not too young or old to be successful at whatever you put your mind to. We are conditioned to believe that things should look a certain way on a specific timeline, when in reality someone else's timeline is irrelevant to our life. We don't have to buy into it. Whoever said that you have to start college at eighteen years of age? What's wrong with fifty-five or fifteen years old if it's the right time for the individual? In most instances, we have the freedom to choose our own timeline.

But if you don't begin to delve deeper into the underlying issue, you may always feel that you're too young or too old to bring your vision to life. Here are a few questions to help process these feelings when you find yourself in a place of doubt because of your age:

- Why does age matter to you?
- Why would it possibly matter to your potential clients/customers?
- And what are the facts to back this up? For example, are there studies out there that support your fear? Most likely not.
- Did someone make a negative comment about your age?
- What story or belief are you replaying that's contributing to your doubts around your qualifications or capabilities?

Going back to that client, I challenged her first with this question: "Is life experience necessary in order to successfully serve your client?" She timidly answered no. And I assured her that life experience was irrelevant in this case. I even pointed out that I was younger than her, yet she still entrusted me to help her navigate her business. Through this conversation, she uncovered that a former potential client had commented that she sounded young, which caused her to internalize doubts about her age and capabilities.

How to Feel Qualified Like a Boss

Here are my words of wisdom for you: You are an expert, and you are qualified exactly where you are. You may not believe it right now. You may be chasing a certification, degree, or higher level of education because you feel you *need* it—but the reality is that you may only *need* it if you *want* it. If it's something you really want to acquire because it feels fun for you to learn, then by all means go for it. But if you think you need it to experience success, I encourage you to dig a little deeper. There is nothing in this moment that you need in order to be successful; you are exactly where you are supposed to be. If that's hard for you to accept, here is a visualization that has been pretty impactful for me while working through this belief. It's one I do with all my clients, and I recommend that you snap a photo of the next couple of paragraphs and keep it stored on your phone so that you can pull it up when the lies creep in.

Get into a comfortable position. Turn off all electronics and close your eyes to begin. Imagine a ten-story ladder. You are climbing the ladder. Above you are the mentors you look up to and the places you want to be, which may feel light-years away. Below you on the ladder is someone just a few steps behind you on a similar journey. They might be close to where you were a year ago. Your mentor reaches their hand down to pull you up, and as you climb higher, you grab the hand of the person right under you and pull them up. Your journey is like climbing a ladder, and just by living, you're acquiring new knowledge and expertise. Little by little you are being supported. You learn, you implement, you begin to master new things, and then you have skills to offer support and share what you have learned.

This process is never ending. We continually strive to be better and do better and become better with each day we are alive. Yet we don't put things on hold while we wait to climb higher—we have skills to give and things to offer in the place we're at today. We are qualified as we are, *and* we are constantly learning new things. Your present self is always more capable than your past self, simply because you have learned through your challenges and experiences. You, my friend, are *already* an expert. You have something that someone else has yet to find. You are the perfect age to begin this journey. You are qualified exactly as you are, without needing anything else. Embrace it. Be proud of it. And make sure to celebrate it!

Just Do the Opposite

Derived from Dialectical Behavior Therapy or DBT, this next skill, *opposite action*,[1] encourages you to do the opposite of what you feel naturally inclined to do. So in the instance of fear, we most naturally freeze, tense up, avoid, or run. Here are a few thought processes you may relate to that I often hear from my clients:

- I am too old to begin my speaking career, so why say yes to that opportunity? I'd rather let someone else take it.
- I only have six out of the eight qualifications requested for the opportunity I would like to try for, so why would I be selected? There is no sense in applying.

- I'd love to submit an application for the ad I saw for a speaking gig, but I know most of the current speakers are older and more seasoned in the field. I'd rather let someone else take it.

These three examples illustrate limiting mindsets. In these instances, each of the women ruled out the opportunity because of limited thinking around age and qualifications. When practicing opposite action, however, I encourage the women to dive into their fear—to do immediately what scares them. The reason for this is because we know that the longer fear hangs out in our mind, the greater our tendency to build it up and turn it into a big to-do. Also, the longer fear lingers, the more brain space it occupies. And who's got time for that?

So consider the opposite action for those three scenarios above:

- I may feel old to begin my speaking career, but why say no to that opportunity? If I don't start today, I may never begin.
- I have all but two of the qualifications they are looking for, so why not apply? The worst they can say is no, but they could say yes based on everything else I've accomplished.
- I know most who speak at that event are older and more seasoned in the field, but why not apply? Maybe they would like the attendees to hear from a variety of people at different stages in life, which would mean I'd get to begin my speaking career at twenty-five years of age.

Opposite action will help you achieve your goals—and save you a lot of stress and time as well. Going back to that last example of feeling too young to be a speaker, here's a scenario you may find yourself in: You are feeling way too young and underqualified to speak at the next local lady boss networking event. Applications are due in a month. Rather than applying right away and seeing what happens, you let it snowball. Each day over the next three weeks you tell yourself you are too young and underqualified. Each time you think this, the doubt grows bigger and stronger in your mind. You've almost fully convinced yourself that you'll never do it, but something comes over you and you decide to just apply for the heck of it. The following week you get an email with an invitation to not only speak but also be a paid speaker.

How would this situation have been different if you had used opposite action from the start? You would have saved a heck of a lot of time. Looking back, worrying about whether to apply held a whole lot of space and thought in your mind for those three weeks. You also would have slept better knowing you had taken the leap in applying and let go of the outcome— the rest was out of your hands! And you wouldn't have been as on edge with your partner and the people around you because your mind would have been free from fighting doubts and deliberating about what to do.

Not only would things have been easier for you, you would have gotten the exact same result! How crazy is that? Imagine if you had applied for the speaking gig the day you saw the ad and spared yourself all of that self-inflicted misery? Now look back on your life and imagine all the time and even heartache you could have saved if you had run toward the opportunities that scared you rather than away from them. Keep this method in mind as other opportunities arise, and begin small. Run toward the small things first, and little by little apply this method to the bigger opportunities in your life.

Willingness Makes Us Qualified

You will hear me say this over and over again: you are exactly who you are supposed to be in this very moment. You are not too much, too little, overqualified, underqualified, too young, too old, too damaged, or too far gone. Don't let anyone ever tell you *who you are* in this moment, and don't you for a second believe that you aren't qualified either. What is meant for you today doesn't require any more preparation than you've already had.

Each and every new door that has opened in my life has been accompanied by doubts that I wasn't old enough or qualified enough or prepared enough—and yet I've stepped forward anyway. I don't have a business or marketing degree, but I've had discernment to navigate my steps in creating a profitable business. I never finished that writing minor I set out to get in college, yet I've embraced the vision and developed the grit to write this book. I'm not qualified to be a mom and teach my daughters how to live healthy lives (it's something so foreign to me), yet day by day I'm learning healthier living habits.

Now wouldn't it be freeing if we could say we're actually not qualified to do any of this, but our willingness to try makes us qualified? I want you to hold on to all the tips you learned in this chapter, but ultimately remind yourself that being qualified to do the thing is less about your abilities and more about your trust in yourself and the vision you have for your life. Ladies, hold on to this and take it with you wherever you go in your life and business. I promise it will save you a lot of hardship!

LIE #4

I Will Never Have Enough Money

'm leaving. I found another job that will pay more and provide more flexible hours. You may not agree, but I believe that I deserve more." After speaking these words to my boss, I turned and fled her office, tears stinging my eyes. I felt like I had just had an out-of-body experience. I had practiced those lines in front of the mirror, and I couldn't believe I'd finally said them aloud. It took everything in me to stand up for my worth—but I knew I had to. For the longest time I felt powerless in my career—but as soon as I realized that no one was going to care about my success as much as I did, something shifted. I realized that because I believed I would never have enough money, my life was playing out in accordance with that belief. I became determined to own what I believed I was worth and speak up for myself and my fellow female colleagues. Without the experience of feeling undervalued in the workplace, I would have stayed complacent with a salary providing just enough to cover the bills, living paycheck to paycheck. And I wouldn't have begun this quest to find my worth, claim it, and get out of the mindset that I will never have enough money.

Does this story resonate with you? Are you in a place today of feeling you don't have enough money, or in a place where you're fearing money? Are you living a life crippled with fear, worrying that you don't have enough, and wondering how the next bills will be paid? You may cringe when you see the postman dropping envelopes at your door or when your email inbox chimes, anticipating the arrival of the next bill, which you may or may not be able to pay. If you are like many female entrepreneurs, chances are that you're living in a scarcity (or lack) mindset, feeling you don't and may never have enough. It's a common way of approaching the world, especially when you're striving to build something new and don't have the financial stability you crave—but it's a debilitating belief that will ultimately keep you from your dreams.

A 2015 survey by the American Psychological Foundation[1] revealed that money was the leading cause of stress among Americans and, surprisingly, even among millionaires. Here's the truth: No matter how much you earn or have in your bank account, if you carry the belief that "I don't have enough money," you will never feel like you have enough money. If you operate from a mindset of scarcity, earning a million dollars will not satisfy you (and could potentially lead to even more problems). In this chapter, we will sort through the most common effects of this scarcity mindset and then turn our energy toward internalizing a mindset of abundance.

I've Never Had Enough Money, and I Don't Believe I Ever Will

The rapper Drake says it best: "Started from the bottom, now I'm here." Ladies, in all seriousness, if Drake started from the bottom and became the musician we know him as today, who are we to say that we can't also achieve the things we set out to do?

I so often hear women using the "I started at the bottom with nothing" (cough, cough) as a way to sabotage what they are capable of achieving. You may be in this mindset today. You—perhaps unwittingly—are using your circumstance as a barrier to making your dreams a reality. You believe that because you had it hard financially early in life or because you are about to go bankrupt today, you are not cut out for financial success in your business. I am happy to break it to you that you, my friend, are wrong. This may sound crazy, but in many ways, those who have had a rough financial upbringing or who start their business from nothing are at an even larger *advantage*. Ever wonder how people who have even less than you survive and make do with what they have? It's because of their creativity. As humans, we will do whatever it takes to survive.

This type of mindset is discussed in one of my all-time favorite books, *The Power of Broke*, by Daymond John.[2] You may know Daymond as a star from the hit television show *Shark Tank*. In his book, he tells stories of self-made millionaires who started from absolutely nothing. Some were homeless, some on welfare, and for each, the odds of becoming a millionaire were 100 percent *against* them. However, they learned to get creative with the little bit that they had. Rather than allow the mindset "I've never had enough money" to hold them back, they found ways to work around it. For example, Daymond saved up enough money to buy a van and drove his friends around to earn a few extra dollars. Then he used that van to sell the first T-shirts he designed. Little by little, using resourcefulness and leveraging each new business, he was able to build what we see today as his FUBU clothing empire. Each story in this book tells of beginnings that were certainly harder than most, where individuals searched hard to find resources that people with money wouldn't take the time to look into.

I started my first business living paycheck to paycheck. I didn't have the means to invest in a course or schooling to learn how to start a business, but I was resourceful and devoured all that I could find for free on the internet. Yes, it took extra time, but it helped me create a business that afforded me the opportunity to quit my nine-to-five. And with the overflow from that first business, I was able to create a second business that produced multiple six figures in revenue over the next few years, all while working part time.

I could have easily believed I needed more money to get started. But I decided to work with what I already had and see what could happen. For those looking in, it might have looked easy, but I was very strategic with my first move to quit my nine-to-five. First, I joined a direct-sales jewelry company. I used this as a way to bring in extra income (a few hundred per month) by hosting jewelry parties in friends' homes. Strategically, these parties connected me with new networks of people with whom I could share my new business. And second, I was able to leave my job quickly because I was used to living paycheck to paycheck on a very small social work salary. So in order to take the leap and leave my job, I didn't need to make much money to replace it.

I wanted to make this happen as if I didn't have a spouse to support me. I opened up a business credit card and made purchases on it one at a time. Yes, I might have been able to ask friends or family to help me out, but it felt good for me to do this on my own! If you do have others helping you, there is zero shame in this whatsoever. We all have differing levels of comfort and desires when creating our businesses.

Your dream is *not* dependent on your bank account. You do not need a lot of money in your hands to start a business or see your business multiply. The same is true even if you grew up at a financial advantage—that doesn't mean you won't struggle with this lie. Regardless of where you come from, you are capable of succeeding. Remember that by being resourceful and intentional with what we do have, we can grow it into so much more.

I Don't Have Enough Money, and I Can Only Be Happy When I Have More

Wealth is a mindset. You could be the richest person in the world but have yet to experience wealth. You could also have very little in life and consider yourself wealthy because of the love and support around you. I am going to start with a few questions for those of you who struggle with feeling that the more money you have, the more content you will be:

- Have you ever felt content with money?
- Was there a time in your past when you would have dreamed you would earn what you are earning today?
- Was there a time in your past when you were earning more than you are earning today and you wish you had relaxed and been content with that amount?

Here is the harsh reality: I'm not sure if anyone truly feels 100 percent content with what they have. Whether you're a six-figure earner desiring to double your income or a stay-at-home mom looking to make extra spending cash, we all have that one thing in common: desiring more in order to someday be content. No matter where we are, we always want to move up to the next level.

Wanting to advance financially isn't a bad thing in and of itself. Having the drive and desire to do more and earn more can be a powerful tool when it comes to business. But when we place the desire for more money as the ultimate goal—telling ourselves that we can only be happy if we get to that next financial figure—it can sabotage both our business success and our happiness.

With this mindset, we often begin to associate being content financially with happiness. *Money will solve my problems, and as a result I will be happy.* With this particular mindset we can miss the goodness of what we already have. This mindset can begin to seep into other areas of life, leaving us discontented with our spouse or our business partner. The more we long for an increase in money, the more the beautiful things around us just don't quite feel like enough.

So how do we separate healthy desire to move forward from unhealthy longing for wealth that won't satisfy? Let's explore the effects of this mindset through writing prompts and a guided visualization.

1. Is there a longing or void in your life that you are trying to fill with money?

   _____

2. Why do you feel more money will bring you greater contentment?

   _____

3. What do you believe money will do for you? What emotion will it bring?

_____

4. Go back to that earlier question: Have you ever felt content with money? Sit with this question for a moment and explore your money story—the relationship you've had with money as a child, young adult, and today. I suggest you take about ten minutes to write whatever comes to mind, free from censoring.

_____

_____

_____

_____

_____

Now that I've asked you to get vulnerable and write your money story out, it is only fair to give you a quick glimpse of mine. I can remember back to those days of earning less. I would daydream what it would be like to make ten thousand more than I was making and then twenty and thirty and eventually doubling my income. I would sit in my little 250-square-foot New York City studio apartment and daydream about fancy dinners out with my boyfriend, monthly spa treatments, and having all the latest and greatest fashions from Bloomies. Ladies, true story. These were all the things that I *thought* would make me content if I had enough money for them. *Once I get to this level of lifestyle, I will feel content. I will feel important. People will take me more seriously.*

Can anyone relate?

Now let's quickly dive into a visualization exercise to help you better understand your own viewpoint.

Close your eyes and think about all of those things that money can buy that you've been dreaming of having. How will your life really be different if you have those things? How will you feel? Do you think people will want to be your friend or have greater respect for you? Will those things really fill the void you're feeling, or could it potentially leave you feeling worse because you'll now realize those things don't bring true contentment?

Money is a super-sensitive subject, and I want to assure you that it's perfectly normal if you find this exercise stirring up some emotions for you. There is nothing wrong with having nice things, but if these nice things are there to fill a void, it can become an issue. I didn't want fancy clothes and handbags just because; I wanted them because I believed that once I had the income to afford them, I would feel better about myself and content with my life. Sound familiar? What void are you trying to fill today? Outside of money, what do you really crave more of in your life? Greater relationship satisfaction? A more fulfilling extracurricular life? Feeling more connected to community?

I've realized that more money does not equal contentment, but relationship satisfaction and acceptance of ourselves does. It took me many years of uncovering these voids to understand that money and things were not actually what I was seeking. Between therapy, practicing tools from DBT, and reading numerous self-help books, I have been able to work through, process, and break free from the need to have these things. Today, over ten years later, by choice I am not living the lifestyle that I thought would make me feel content and fulfilled. The income has increased substantially, but I don't need all of those things to make me happy.

Does any of this resonate with you today? Do you ever fantasize about having a certain amount of money because you believe this will bring you contentment? Take a moment for reflection. What void really needs to be filled? What can you begin working on to provide yourself with more satisfaction in life? Once you implement these tools and begin to discover the core of what you really want, I promise that some of those current material desires will fade away.

I Believe I Don't Have Enough Money, and So I Can't Be Generous

Believing that we need more money to be happy is one dangerous outgrowth of a scarcity mindset. Another is the belief that we don't have enough and therefore must cling to what we do have. At its core, a scarcity mindset kills our ability to be generous. Time after time I've heard some version of this statement: "I don't think I have enough and therefore I can't be generous. I need to feed my family first. I need to pay my bills first. If I give money to charity or other causes, I won't have enough to pay my staff. My business expenses won't be paid if I give, and eventually I'll have no business."

These scenarios are very real. Many of you may be experiencing financial hardship. I worked with the homeless for a year during my graduate studies, and some of those clients were the most generous people I have ever met. Many of them had such a beautiful generosity mindset, and I share this because no one should ever feel excluded from giving based on their present circumstances.

Now I'll be the first to admit I have had second thoughts on whether I wanted to donate during a financially stretching season, but I've adapted a mindset that my life and business cannot afford to *not* give. If I want to show gratitude for the abundance I have received, it's important that I give back a portion of what's been provided to me. And I repeat, *give back*. Giving is a simple act of acknowledging what you *have* and a willingness to share this with others.

So why do so many of us still feel torn about giving even when we know that we want to support others? This mindset typically boils down to scarcity thinking: *I believe I don't have enough and if I give to others, that means I'll have even less than I already have*. When we look at it that way, it does sound scary, similar to *having* to pay our bills or taxes when money already feels tight! But giving doesn't have to be this way.

Back in January of 2016 I surrendered this scarcity mindset and have never looked back. I was a full year into being completely on my own in business, free from a nine-to-five. Up until then I gave to organizations when I felt I had the extra money—and as we know, many of us never feel like we have extra; there is always another bill to pay. I was newly into my second business, and income was still pretty sporadic.

One day I sat on my couch looking at my bank statement on the computer screen, stressing about how I would ever get ahead on the bills. I decided to do what I do when I'm stuck—I prayed for guidance. Something that I wasn't expecting happened. I was hoping to find some peace and comfort, but instead, I felt a nudge to take what I had (the little bit) and donate it to a particular cause. And to be perfectly honest, I really didn't want to. I mean, who wants to take the little bit of money that they have, not even enough to cover the bills, and give it away? It almost felt irresponsible of me to do this. I was always the type of person who paid all my bills on time and hated owing anyone money, but I felt I needed to take a risk. I felt uneasy giving beyond my means, yet I still went ahead and donated and even put my bank account on monthly auto-pay for this recurring amount.

Here's the amazing part: after doing so, I went to check my email for the confirmation to bookmark, and I noticed an email from PayPal. I opened it, and I kid you not, it was a bank deposit for a few dollars OVER what I had just donated. I had booked a brand-new client for a new coaching package I had recently introduced in my business. Tears began streaming down my face in awe of this confirmation. The lie that I carried with me for years of not having enough money to give to others was instantly lifted. From that day forward I carried the mindset that I will always have enough, and there is no reason to live with a scarcity mindset.

After this experience, I decided to do something some may view as a little radical. I realized that the number I had given that year was a little over 10 percent of what my huge, stretching, yearly money goal was. That day I made a declaration that each year I will give 10 percent of whatever my money goal might be—divided into monthly payments—even if I am not earning that amount just yet. I felt a strong pull to trust that I will always be taken care of. For me, this was an act of letting go and surrendering, and I felt completely at peace moving forward. My mindset shifted from *I don't have this amount to give*, to *Even if I end up giving over 10 percent of my income, this is a beautiful thing. And on the other hand, if I end up making more than what I had anticipated, I will simply get to give more at the end of the year!* I now was saying, I *get* to give and no longer I *have to, need to,* or *should* give out of obligation.

To this day, this has been my outlook on giving. I am sharing this as an example of what I personally do *today*. This doesn't mean this is how I will give forever, and it certainly doesn't mean that this is the only right way or how *you* should give. Through this experience, I have been able to approach money in a different way. Even when there are seasons when money is a little tighter, I find that this approach has completely shifted my mindset toward money.

What is your generosity story? Take some time and write it out below. And please, ladies, remember this is shame and judgment free! Just because this hasn't been a priority for you in the past doesn't mean that you now "owe" others or need to add up all your lifetime income and make up for lost giving. It doesn't work that way—there should never be guilt associated with giving.

If you feel the desire to give to charitable organizations, what will this giving journey look like? How will you begin shifting your money mindset and showing your commitment? Take some time to write about it in the space below—and remember, each of us has a different giving story and perspective. Yours is yours and mine is mine. Really take some time to reflect and open your heart to what feels good for you. But before you dive in, take a moment and meditate on these mantras:

- No gift is too small to make an impact on someone else's life.
- What may feel like little for you is often what someone else needs for a miracle to happen.
- Open hands to give are always open to receive.

My generosity story:

_____

_____

_____

_____

_____

_____

More Than Mindset

Okay, so we've covered just how detrimental this scarcity mindset can be to your business and your life and looked at some ways to overcome that mentality. I'd like to end this chapter by giving you a few ways to easily find or earn extra money. My husband and I have relied on these tricks a number of times, and we always find that we end up with a little more in the bank when we do.

Utilize the Google Search Bar

We live in a day and age where information is readily available. Can't afford that course or coaching program you feel is essential to get you to that next level? Most paid courses and programs offer a plethora of free trainings that will help you out. Keep in mind that almost all free trainings will lead to some sort of sales pitch, but most of the time it's worth it for the free help! The reason that extensive courses and programs cost money is because they provide you with an advantage—condensing all of the information into a nice little package to save you time and eventually money. But again, most of the information in any course you will take isn't revolution-ary, and if you search long and hard, it's accessible and free somewhere on the internet. And just so you know, even much of the content in my courses can be found for free if you do some searching.

Sell, Sell, Sell

Get rid of stuff you no longer need. We all have stuff hang-ing around the house that we aren't using. According to a study conducted by Nielson Customized Research, the average family has around three thousand dollars in unused stuff in their homes.[3] Last week I went and picked up a ninety-seven-dollar check from my local consignment shop. Score! Ladies, this is basically free money. I had stuff shoved in the back of my closet that I was no longer wearing. If you have other household items you want to sell, you can even have a garage sale. You know what they say: one man's junk is another man's treasure!

Fiscal Fast

A fiscal fast is when you set a goal to stop spending money for a period of time. My first time doing this was several Christ-mases ago when I was working in New York City as a social worker with very little money to buy gifts. I decided I would try to make Christmas gifts with what I already had. This equated to homemade granola, crocheted infinity scarves, and Star-bucks coffee purchased with credit card points. I decorated my little Brooklyn one-bedroom apartment (yep, I'd upgraded since my first story in the book!) with a three-dollar miniature Christmas tree from the Goodwill store and paper chain decorations I made from Trader Joe's brown paper bags—which I kept and still hang up every year to remind me of how far I've come. During this fiscal fast, I made it a point to eat up whatever was in my cupboards or freezer, to get super thrifty with buying only a few fresh things so that my meals were still nutritious, and to not spend any money during that time unless I used gift cards that were lying around. Warning: you'll feel like you're back in college, but it is 100 percent worth it. I did this for a month and saved several hundred dollars that I wouldn't have if I hadn't done it.

Practice Gratitude

Now, this last point wasn't going to be here, but as I was editing this chapter in front of the fireplace with my newborn sleeping on my chest and Christmas music in the background, I heard one of my favorites from the old Bing Crosby movie *White Christmas*, which reminded me that gratitude is everything! When we truly aren't feeling like we have enough money, go back to the lyrics of this song and REFLECT: "When my bankroll is getting small/ I think of when I had none at all/And I fall asleep counting my blessings."[4] Melody Beattie states, "Gratitude unlocks the fullness of life. It turns what we have into enough, and more."[5] My tip for you is to think back on a time that it felt impossible to survive financially and reflect on how you are still standing. You still have a place to lay your head at night. You still had something to eat this week. You still have the space to do something enjoyable like read this book. You can be grateful for where you are today *and* celebrate where you are going in the future.

LIE #5

Making Money Is Greedy

always believed in abundance. But even with this belief, there was a small part of me that attached guilt to receiving anything monetary. Up until just the last few years, my thought process typically looked something like this: *I am grateful for all that I have, and I don't want to be greedy. There are many things I would love to have and achieve, and it would mean so much to me if I could experience even some of the things that I dream of. But I really don't need all of my desires to be fulfilled—maybe just one would be nice.*

It sounds humble, perhaps, but ladies, the truth is that this is an intention from someone who doesn't believe she is worthy for the floodgates to fully open to abundance. Abundance can mean a lot of things—business success, wealth, health, children—but in this chapter, I want to focus specifically on abundance in terms of money. We've already talked quite a bit about money and the danger that it can pose to us when we operate out of a mindset of scarcity. But what about the other side of the coin—where we feel ashamed and greedy wanting more?

In the example above, I'm sure you can hear the shame I felt in wanting too much. I worried about being greedy. I worried about being too concerned with financial matters. For much of my career, I even felt that desiring multiple opportunities, specifically ones that could lead to increased income, meant that I would be robbing from others. As we will see over the course of this chapter, when you are in a good money mindset you don't doubt or question how much you are capable of receiving—you request what it is you desire, and you allow what is meant for you to find you.

In that season I was believing and working toward a number of things, but I was only giving a halfhearted attempt. What do I mean? Well, here are the five specific things I was believing for:

1. A podcast. The confidence to finally make it happen. I knew that having a podcast could not only be a resource to others, but also help send potential clients my way for greater abundance.

2. An intern I could train and mentor. I wanted to practice leading and thinking bigger in my business by onboarding women who believe in my mission just as much as I do. This would also allow me to bless these students with some extra money for their tuition or whatever they need it for.

3. An agent for my book. Writing books could be another small stream of income and a way to reach even more women at an accessible price point.

4. Financial abundance so that I could fully commit to taking at least three full months with my new baby girl, plus space to write my book. And ladies, I actually wrote down a number of how much I needed to earn to be able to cover my bills, still donate to organizations the full amount I was when earning, and maybe leave a little cushion in case I wanted to hire some extra help in my business.

5. And the stretch goal: a signed publishing contract before the baby arrived.

Now these were huge and very specific intentions for me. I felt greedy even admitting I wanted them all. Are you in a season today where you can relate? You have financial goals you would like to hit—ones that feel huge and maybe even "too much"? Maybe you are believing for more money so that you can start a family. You may be believing for direction in how you can begin earning more money by working less so that you have time to spend with your family. You dream of creating enough income to transition your husband out of his life-draining job and into your business. You haven't been on a vacation with your girlfriends in years and would love a monthly surplus to add to this vacation fund. And maybe you want all of these things.

I can already hear the inner chatter: *No way. I am not worthy. Who am I to ask for even half of these things? I've already been fortunate. Why should I want more?* Have similar words ever crossed your mind? I bet they have. And when these mindsets are present, they sure play out in our businesses, with our clients, with our collaborations, and with those we hope to serve in the future.

Now before I share with you how I managed to let go of my fear and boldly began welcoming and working toward abundant opportunity, let's break apart some of the most common sub-lies we tell ourselves when it comes to money and business.

I Feel Greedy Selling

So many of us associate shame with sales. When you think of selling, you cringe, imagining yourself on one of those cheesy radio commercials selling used cars. Though I will say that not all used car salesmen are the same. I found and purchased my "mom car" from the loveliest used car salesman. (Ladies, I drive a Ford F150 super cab pickup truck. Go ahead, imagine five-foot-four me trying to get in—you have permission to laugh!) And of course I recommend him to everyone, because he is the exact opposite of the stereotype. Anyway, if you feel icky selling, you're definitely not alone—but are you aware of how this attitude has negatively affected you in business?

Here's the thing: Money is just an exchange of energy. An exchange of trust. And an exchange of commitment. When

A QUICK NOTE: Throughout this chapter I will use the phrase *an abundance of money*. This phrase will mean something different for each of you reading it. Some of you may view an extra $200 as an abundance of money, and for some, $200,000 will come to mind when I say these words. Either way, it's all the same thing—an amount that is above what we already have and also feels slightly reachable. Whatever that number is for you, hold on to the idea of what abundance means for you.

people physically hand over their credit card, they are making a declaration that they believe they will receive something of value. And in order to do this, to physically hand over the plastic, they must first acknowledge belief in themselves in this way:

- If I purchase this new system for my business, I will energetically be available to invest time into learning how to use it.
- If I pay a business consultant to help me start my business, I will energetically be available to put her strategies into action.
- If I pay for a mindset coach to help me navigate my fears around sales calls, I will energetically be available to do the work so that I can receive a return on my investment.

Again, when people are ready to pay for our products or services, they are declaring that they are ready to receive. And when we are uncomfortable accepting money or feel weird around sales, people sense our unsteady energy. When this happens, we actually end up repelling potential customers. Then we wonder, *Why aren't people buying from me? I don't understand. I have an amazing product. I'm the most honest person out there.* This may be true, but your lack of confidence in selling will repel people

Before we can shift our thinking around sales, we must uncover where the mindset that selling is bad, embarrassing, sleazy, or shameful is rooted. The best way to do this is to pull out a journal or piece of paper and start writing. Write down the first things that come to mind when you hear the word "sales." Do not overthink this. Actually, don't think at all, just write. You want to make sure when you participate in this exercise that you are not censoring yourself. After you write down your sales associations, ask yourself, *How is this story not serving me, and also, how is it serving me?*

Here are a few questions I ask my clients, which you may find useful as well:

- Have you always felt selling was bad? When did this mindset begin?
- Did someone once tell you it was greedy to sell?
- Have you had a bad experience buying from someone?
- Did an experience with a potential client drive you to feel this way?
- How has this impacted your business?
- Where would your business be if this limited thinking could be removed?

Done? Good! Now hold on to these sales associations while we dive into a couple of pointers to help you switch this embedded belief.

In order to let go of the guilt and shame you may associate with selling—and to therefore become *good* at it—you need to switch your perspective. To best serve your customers, you must believe that the selling you're doing is beneficial, for the good of others, and will benefit those who buy your product. This shift will help build your confidence, making sales and money actually enjoyable for you and the receiving party. There are two quick shifts that will help.

First, keep in mind that if you don't make the sale, someone else will. If you are questioning your intentions around money or feeling greedy accepting money from others, please know this: you, my friend, are not the least bit greedy. You are kind. You are generous. You care about others' well-being. You have high integrity. And you are probably in this for the right reasons. I know it with all my heart, because a heart of greed would never attach guilt or shame to the exchange of money. Know that if you don't get out and start making sales, you will miss out on opportunities to help people who really need you.

Hold on tightly to this mantra: "It is my responsibility in this world to become comfortable at sales so that I can empower others to make informed decisions with their money." After this clicked for me, I instantly began experiencing guilt *not* selling to people. I knew that by selling my services, my customers would get the highest quality care.

Second, offer brownies. Ladies, I love me some brownies— warm, gooey, with crispy edges, and extra chocolate chips. And when I see a brownie, I want it. No circumstance will change the fact that I will never decline a brownie. (And if you're one of those crazy people who *don't* like them—not to worry; we can still be friends, just more brownies for me!) Now, how do brownies and sales go hand in hand?

Close your eyes and get all your senses ready for this visualization: It's a crisp fall day. You're sitting in the bleachers of your old high school with friends for the annual homecoming game. In your lap is a big tin of brownies you brought straight from the oven. You open it, grab one, take a big bite, and what comes next? Do you eat the entire tin of brownies yourself? Or do you turn to your friends, maybe even some of the strangers sitting around you, and offer them a brownie? I know I sure would! Your friends are most likely comfortable asking for one and may even grab one. But the surrounding people who don't know you may not ask for a brownie unless you offer.

If you're anything like me and have your hands on a good thing, you want to share it with everyone. You turn around and ask your old chemistry teacher if she would like a brownie. She informs you she has a gluten and egg allergy and sadly declines. You ask the group of ladies sitting below you. Three out of the six don't hesitate, and have devoured theirs before the other three have told you their reasons for not accepting one (one is on the Whole30 diet, another has a dairy allergy, and the last one doesn't like chocolate. Come on, who doesn't like chocolate?). Simple math—out of the seven people, three accepted your invitation and four had differing reasons for declining, which were completely understandable.

And this is sales. You have a whole lot of a good thing. You want to share it with the world, not because you're greedy, but because you have a heart for sharing a good thing when you get your hands on it. *Offering* that good thing is not pushy or manipulative. It is simply asking a question, placing the offer in the other person's lap, and giving them the freedom to accept or not. Here's the thing: if you never asked that group of women, zero out of the seven would have received your chocolate blessing. But because you were confident in your product, you decided to *invite*, and in turn, three accepted.

What if you could begin viewing sales through this new lens? What if you believed that it is your responsibility to offer ethical services and products—that by *not* offering, you are actually keeping others from a good thing. It's simply an invitation. Rather than greedy, can you see that it is in fact generous—sharing with others the blessings you have to offer? As you begin to view sales this way, I assure you that in time, the "feeling greedy" mindset will dissipate.

I Feel Greedy Accepting Money Because This Is a Calling

As women, we may feel an even greater hesitation to sell products and earn money if we view our businesses as a calling—something that we do to impact and give back to others.

Let me note that this section speaks to two different types of callings: First is a traditional nonprofit organization. For example, my friend Elisabetta Colabianchi founded a 501(c)3 organization to help provide education to girls in Mozambique. Helping young women have access to education is near and dear to my heart and a mission that my business gives back to. Second is running a business not only to generate an income but to have a positive impact and create a ripple effect in this world. This applies to those of you who view your business interaction with others as a calling and even a representation of your belief system. Most of the women I work with fall into this category.

Traditional Nonprofit Organizations

Let's begin with those in traditional nonprofit organizations. I often hear from them the limiting belief that they are greedy if they accept money for work that is a calling. Ladies, I have an interesting perspective for you. I grew up as a pastor's kid, and I can tell you—money is imperative for any type of organization's sustainability. My parents both worked full-time jobs and had side jobs in order to support our family in the early days of my dad taking on a position of senior pastor at a new church. This resulted in my parents being stretched too thin, which left very little time to spend as a family, and my father experienced numerous medical issues due to stress. In order for them to continue serving and pouring into the people, it became clear that he needed to begin taking some sort of salary to lessen the projects he had on the side. My father couldn't handle the entire financial burden himself; he would burn out and, in turn, wouldn't have the capacity to lead.

Friend, the same goes for you. You cannot run an organization effectively unless there is an exchange of money. How well can it actually be run if you are burning the candle at both ends—perhaps working another job to pay the bills because you have yet to be paid by your organization or are not taking enough of a salary? Or perhaps you're agonizing about asking others to donate to your organization or about fundraising your salary, telling yourself that this is a calling and so you shouldn't benefit financially in any way. There is only so long you can continue at this rate. In order for you to show up as the best version of yourself in all areas of life, work, business, and organization, you need room for margin. And money, my friend, will give you just that.

Something I learned from my friend Kelly Lyndgaard, founder of Unshattered, an organization that employs women in recovery, is that in order for an organization to secure funding to expand its reach, it is crucial that the CEO receives compensation. Kelly explained that when she began Unshattered, she chose not to draw a salary for her work. However, she says, "I'm finding as we grow, that Foundations and Donors are concerned that the organization does not have a paid CEO. From their perspective, they see this as a liability because in the event that the organization needed to replace me, there is not a salary built in to the budget."[1] So not only is it important for *you* to earn money while running an organization, but it is also important for the future of your organization and employees.

I know it might feel uncomfortable accepting more money, but trust me, you will show up as your best leader self if you receive compensation for the time and energy you invest. If you are having a hard time asking for donations for your organization, get creative. There are so many ways for people to raise money these days: Start a crowdfunding page and ask people you know to donate. Host an in-person fundraiser to cultivate community, spread your message, and raise the needed funds. Search your local community for grant opportunities.

I love how my friend Elisabetta funds her organization, Kurandza. She partners with other female business owners who want to make an impact (without needing to start a non-profit) by essentially giving them the role of a brand ambassador. As a brand ambassador they commit to supporting your mission by spreading your message and giving a portion of their business sales to your organization. The sky is the limit. The key to funding your organization in this way is to reject feelings of guilt in the process. Again, like the brownies, you are inviting others to partake in an opportunity, not forcing them. If it aligns with their values and they are in the financial space to donate, they will. And if it's not the best timing for them, they can simply decline. It's as easy as that.

Businesses That Make an Impact and Generate Income

Now another person I want to speak to is the entrepreneur who views their actual business as a calling—which if you are reading this book, could quite possibly be you. If you view your business as a calling, chances are that you feel guilty making money from it—or at least making "too much" money. You may own a photography studio or a coffee shop and see each client or customer as an opportunity to show kindness and encouragement and to be a light to those who need it. You may have fears such as: *I will be judged for charging these prices and no longer appear to be a good person*, or, *In order for me to spread kindness in this world, I need to give my services away for free*. Now where did this mindset ever come from? Did someone tell you that in order to be a good person, you must give everything away for free? Again, just like we discussed above with running an actual nonprofit organization, if you are giving it all away for free, you are most likely not taking care of yourself or your family, and in time, you will burn out. In order to be a great business owner, you simply need to serve people well while charging your worth. Serving well and charging your worth are not mutually exclusive. Period.

Now there may be specific circumstances where you feel a nudge to give to someone, and if so, I encourage you to listen to that feeling. One of my clients recently felt her intuition guiding her to gift a photography engagement shoot to a couple who couldn't afford this add-on to their wedding package. Though she was giving away her services for free, she felt abundantly blessed by the gesture: it warmed her heart to do it, and she even mentioned that the bride cried in gratitude when it was offered. Just like donating, giving away our time, services, or goods is not something *we have to do*, but something *we get to do*. Each of us is provided with gifts and talents in our businesses that we can freely give if we choose to. We have the freedom to give, and it blesses us in many ways above and beyond when we do. So whether you have an actual organization or you view your business as a form of calling, remember that money is simply a tool.

I Feel Greedy Earning an Abundance of Money

How much money is too much money? I get this question a lot from my clients, especially from those who report a strong sense of faith or spirituality. If our business is *too* successful, are we somehow inherently greedy? Up until a few years back I used to get really uncomfortable declaring that I wanted to earn more than I was making, and I felt the need to justify such a claim. Do you find yourself doing this? It may look something like this: *I want to make six figures, and if I do, I will give half to charity. I'd feel greedy keeping it, and I'm fine still scraping by to pay my taxes and bills. I don't want to become materialistic or for people to think I'm prideful.*

For some strange reason, many women feel that earning a lot of money needs to be justified. We don't generally hear men talking this way, ladies, do we? I also used to view money through this lens—thinking that "martyr" behavior, such as giving much of what I earned away, equated to being a good person. Many of us fear we will become greedy or that we may grow egocentric with the more money we make. It's a belief that anything above what we already have will change us—and not for the better.

Ladies, here's the simple truth: money is a magnifier of your heart. What is already there will just shine brighter the more you earn. If you are prideful or greedy with little, you will be even more so with a lot. But if you are humble and giving with a little, you will be even more humble and giving with a lot.

When I interviewed global meditation and wellness teacher Cassandra Bodzak on my *Thinking Like a Boss* podcast, she said something that really struck a chord with me: "If you want to know where someone stands with money, it's pretty simple: watch how responsible their hands are with it."[2] Oprah comes to mind when I think of someone who has had an abundance of monetary success. She has earned a great deal of money through her endeavors, and I see her as someone with a giving heart who uses her wealth for good in this world through organizations, charities, programs, etc. In my opinion, people like Oprah are the best people to make an abundance of money because they have responsible hands to nurture and impact the world for the better.

Now that I no longer feel greedy earning money, giving is still a huge part of my business, but—and this may surprise some of you—I am now in the mindset that it doesn't have to be the main focus for why I want to earn money. In fact, that additional money has allowed me to do all kinds of things, including but not limited to giving it to others. The more money I've earned in my business, the more time I've been able to give back. Greater income has afforded me more time and less scarcity around it. Today I am able to take an hour or two out of my day to help someone out or offer something free to someone who really can't afford it. It also helps me be a better mom to my girls, who will someday go and make a difference in this world. If I repelled money away from me because of fears of being perceived as greedy, I wouldn't have the time that I do to pour into my girls and build them up to be strong female leaders. I am also able to outsource business and personal tasks, which provides other women with employment and allows me to feel more at ease with my time. At the end of the day, making money empowers us to do good in the world—as long as we view it as a tool for such.

I want to leave you with a few truths to keep in your pocket for that day you need a reminder or affirming truth.

- A giving heart with little is an even bigger heart when entrusted with a lot.
- In order to make an even greater difference in this world, money needs to be viewed as a tool. The more a business grows, the more money is earned, and the greater reach it has to spread your message. Higher earnings in a business also open more opportunities for jobs and employment for those who need it.
- Money buys you time. You are able to volunteer your time and services when you have an abundance, without needing to second-guess.

Hold on to these truths, ladies, and share them with someone else who may need them in their own season of doubt.

Gaining the Confidence to Ask for Abundance

Now that we have deconstructed each of these sub-lies, I want to share the rest of my story with you. After years of feeling like I couldn't have the desires of my heart without appearing greedy, how did I gain the confidence to boldly believe in abundance? It started with the Colour Conference in April of 2018, where I went seeking clarity and confirmation on one of those five intentions I mentioned in the opening of this chapter. I felt greedy wanting two, let alone all five. But this conference spoke directly to my soul, and something shifted. During one presentation, the speaker, Bobbie Houston, displayed this quote, written by her husband, on the main screen:

> What are your wildest dreams? Your craziest ideas, deepest longings, and grandest plans—the things you've not dared to tell anyone and barely allowed your soul to imagine? I ask because it is exactly that dream, that vision, those grand plans of yours that aren't enough. What a small thinker you are! All of heaven is looking down upon you, shaking their heads, and saying, "*Is that all?! Is that all she wants? Is that all she can dream of?*"
>
> —Brian Houston[3]

And in that moment I received these words: *Daughter, is this all you really want? Is this all that you believe you are capable of receiving?* I felt convicted. Who was I to limit what I was capable of receiving? My dreams were not greedy. My dreams existed because they were implanted within me—and I was entrusted to birth them. These dreams are not mine to keep but gifts for me to share.

When I realized this, I was emboldened to put the intention out there (guilt-free). I prayed that if these gifts were for me, I would have the courage to claim them and the strength to pursue them (a.k.a. do the work, ladies!), and I would be available to receive not one, but all five dreams. And guess what? Within five months, after claiming, doing the gritty work, and opening my hands, I received all five of those intentions, plus a whole lot more. And I happily (free from guilt) accepted them ALL. And because I now had financial peace, I was able to enjoy my time staying home with my precious baby girl the first few months of her life. Today I can donate more than I ever imagined possible. I can chip away at more of my student loans. And I am able to impart more financial peace on others by hiring them to help in my business while I'm on maternity leave. As you can see, seeking to earn more money wasn't an act of greed whatsoever. It was a way for me to expand what was already in my heart. And it's the same for you, my friend—money can be a tool for you to go and live out your mission in this world. Okay, ladies? Now go and offer up those brownies!

LIE #6

I Need to Say Yes to Every Opportunity that Comes My Way

held down the voice record button in my walkie-talkie phone app, unable to contain my enthusiasm as I sent the message to my business coach. "OMG, Amber, I was accepted! This is something I've dreamed about the last couple of years and never thought would be possible for me!"

I was talking about being accepted as an affiliate partner for B-School—an online marketing course created by a woman named Marie Forleo, who has helped successfully launch the careers of countless female entrepreneurs. When I first stumbled across a Facebook ad for Marie's program in 2014, I didn't have a business, and although I had a dream, I wasn't sure if I would ever be capable of designing a thriving business. But I began seeing numerous ads that were run by other successful female entrepreneurs who had taken Marie's B-School course in the past and were now teaming up with her to offer access to her course and bonus content of their own. I was intrigued.

In the coming year I followed along and began consuming any free content Marie released, and in 2015 I took the leap and registered for the course. I can remember waiting until the very last minute to gather the nerve to click the buy button. A flood of thoughts raced through my mind: *What if I pay all of this money and my business fails? What if I invest this money and my business actually succeeds?*

Marie's program had a group of affiliate partners who worked with her to promote the course, and for the longest time I looked at these successful, accomplished women with big dreamy eyes. I wondered what it would be like to make it to a place in business where I would have that kind of opportunity. I told myself, *If I can be in their shoes one day, I will have made it.* At the time, though, it felt like an impossible daydream; something I could never actually achieve.

Well, guess what? In 2017 I took the leap and applied to be an affiliate, was accepted, and eagerly said yes. I couldn't believe it; I began working with my team on a plan to prepare for the big launch. I was shocked, honored, and in complete disbelief that the thing I had dreamed about for so long was actually becoming a reality! But in the midst of all of the excitement and planning, I began to realize that something felt really off. What was this feeling? Was I afraid? Maybe these were just nerves? Or was it something else—was I beginning to recognize that in the midst of all the disbelief and excitement, I had an inner sense that maybe this wasn't actually the best *yes* for this season?

That was a scary idea—I'd never *dreamed* of saying no; as soon as I was accepted, I was all in. But what if that had been . . . a mistake? I attempted to talk myself out of the doubts I was experiencing. Rationally it appeared that I was just feeling like a little fish in a big pond—but deep in my heart I began to understand it was more than that. Back in Lie #2 we discussed intuition, that deep-in-the gut feeling you get when you sense a strong truth. When you have this inner sense and continue to ignore it, you may even feel betrayal and disappointment in yourself. Well, *that's* the feeling I had. But it made no sense. This was the opportunity I had been waiting for. I went back and forth with my marketing team and coach, trying to figure out if I needed to step away from participating in something I'd dreamed of for so long. And no matter what, it just didn't feel aligned. As we talked about in Lie #2, I felt it. You know, that restless feeling that if you don't follow that prompting, you might miss out on something bigger that was meant for you? And this is exactly how fear of missing out hits us. We say yes to something good, but we ultimately miss out on something great and better aligned for our situation.

At the last possible moment to cancel B-School, I decided I was out. I was terrified that I was making a mistake, but I also felt pulled to take space for myself. I was stretched too thin, and I knew it. In this moment I needed to choose risk over comfort. I reached out to the event coordinators right away and informed them I was backing out. They were so kind and gracious to me—but it still really hurt to take back my *yes*. The launch went on, and each time I saw an ad or someone posting about it, I felt major FOMO (you know, ladies, that fear of missing out!). Yet, amazingly, I also felt complete peace in my heart that I had done the right thing.

The Pressure to Say Yes

Have you ever found yourself at a crossroads? Maybe you're there today. You have what feels like an opportunity at your feet that you've been dreaming about for years, but you also feel a sense that the timing isn't quite right. Maybe you find yourself asking, *What happens if I miss this opportunity? Will other opportunities stop coming my way if I don't take them all? Will people be disappointed with me if I don't say yes? Will I never be asked or offered these opportunities again?*

I'm sure you've wrestled with these thoughts, because I have. You find yourself living in a fear-of-missing-out mindset, so you say yes to it all in hopes of not losing out—yet you never feel satisfied with the outcomes. Oftentimes others begin to notice it way before you even do. Because you are doing it all, you find that people aren't as satisfied with your work. They may begin to drop hints here and there, or they may even boldly tell you they are unhappy. People may comment that you look tired, suggest you take some time off, encourage you to outsource more, or even advise you to visit a therapist. As you can see, when this limiting belief is not identified, it creates even bigger problems. It perpetuates, and as a result, you live your life and business in a constant state of disarray. Quantity begins to rule over quality, and because of this, your confidence dips. You begin feeling like you're doing everything, but nothing is being done right. In time, this limiting belief prevents you from running your life and business effectively.

Here's the truth: Saying yes to everything does not make you superwoman, a better friend or family member, or a more serious business owner. Giving in to the pressure to say yes to everything dilutes your effectiveness.

Can you relate to any of this? Do you find yourself running here, running there, forgetting this, forgetting that, not doing anything with excellence, and having to eventually say no to opportunities you really regret missing out on? If so, ladies, you are not alone. This is one of the hardest lies to overcome. It will likely require a change in mindset that you may need to practice again and again. It takes confidence, boundary setting, and a whole lot of getting quiet with yourself.

Oftentimes the things you think are your best yesses in the moment are really just there to teach you a lesson. I learned this concept years ago from my dear aunt Tina after I was having trouble comprehending why something that seemed like an obvious yes ultimately panned out to be a no. What she taught me was that some opportunities may be placed in your life to show you that you will be capable of achieving them at some point in the future. It's imperative that you learn to decipher which yesses are the best yesses and which yesses need to be noes or slows. When you have the clarity to distinguish between these, you will save yourself unnecessary stress and turmoil. Your life and business will be simplified. Before I can offer you the tools to begin giving only your best yesses, we must first tackle the confidence piece. So roll up your sleeves, get ready to face discomfort, and let's dive in!

Confident Decision Making

Though it may not seem obvious, I think that the struggle with whether to say yes is, at its core, a question of confidence. My first question for you is, WHY are you saying yes to everything? Even though we've never met, I can tell you with confidence that you're not saying yes to #allthethings because you actually want to. It's because you think you *should*, or that you *have to*, or that you *need to*, and that you can't confidently say no. Operating from a place of *should*, *have to*, or *need to* will hold you back from being the successful CEO of your life and business. What will get you far is getting still with yourself, diving deep into the stories you've been believing, and then confidently asking yourself, *What is it that I really WANT*? So now my question for you: What opportunities do you want to say yes or no to confidently in your business?

Somewhere along the way we are offered an opportunity that we currently don't have access to. We feel that if we don't take it, we will lose it or lose out forever. If we trace this mindset to its root, we might find that it's been present for a while. Maybe it began in middle school. All of your friends were getting boyfriends, and you felt a slight tinge of missing out. Rather than go to that eighth-grade dance alone, you decided to say yes to the first boy who asked. You didn't really like him, but you also weren't sure if anyone else would ever ask you, so you operated from a place of *I should or else* and then began carrying that mindset into other areas of your life and business.

Do you find yourself operating from a place of *need to*s, *have to*s, or *should*s? When you assess your responsibilities and commitments, do you find that 85 percent of your day consists of things that you thought you *needed to*, *had to*, or *should have* been doing? Do you recognize that a very small piece of your life actually consists of what you *want* to be doing? If this is the case, you are being reactive rather than proactive. It becomes second nature to respond to demands rather than intentionally design your life and business around your values and desires. And this, ladies, is not living from a place of confidence but rather a place of scarcity. If you find yourself falling into this trap of feeling incapable of confidently saying yes or no, here are a few simple ways to flip this mindset:

- When an opportunity arises, ask yourself this question: *If my dream opportunity were presented alongside the offer in front of me, which one would I choose?* Most likely it would be the dream one, right? And if so, ask yourself, *Does this current opportunity align with my dream opportunity down the line? Will this be preparation? Will it open doors to connect me with the right people?* If the answer is yes, then go for it! If no, then I think it's clear you're going to want to say "not now."

- Believe that confidently saying "not now" to something doesn't mean forever. Back in 2017 it was really hard for me to say "not now" to being a part of that B-School launch, but this didn't mean I would never have that opportunity again.

- Be confident that opportunities are always on the way. By saying "not now," you're keeping space open for a better opportunity tomorrow. I honestly can't look back and say I ever regretted saying no to something. Even though it hasn't always been easy, I have only ever felt relief after saying no.

- Believe there is another woman for the job. Most women voice feeling bad about saying no to an opportunity because they may offend the person who offered it. Think of it this way: you stepping into your power and only taking on the things that you want to do allows someone else to potentially have their dream opportunity. It's all about shifting our perspective and looking at the other side of things. So in the future when you are presented with something you know isn't right for you now, there's a chance to suggest someone who may be a great fit. You can connect those two people. I do this all the time: "It's not the best fit for me right now and I actually think I may have someone for you who may even be the better fit for it. If you'd like, I can connect you two." When you say "not now," it will likely give someone else that very opportunity they've been working toward.

Now that you can begin feeling more confident with the act of saying "not now," let's review some boundaries for decision making.

Your Best Yes

If you have difficulty setting boundaries and saying no, it will be challenging to get a firm grip on your best yesses. Boundaries take confidence. Without confidence, boundaries do not exist. So in order to give your best yes, it's imperative you build your confidence and become relentless in all areas of your life and business. In an effort to feel fulfilled and only give our best yesses, it's important to set boundaries in three particular areas: boundaries with others, boundaries in our day-to-day, and boundaries with ourselves.

Let's begin with the hardest one first: *boundaries with ourselves*. Yes, other people attempt to cross our boundaries at times, but more often than not we *allow* them to cross our boundaries because we have yet to set boundaries with ourselves. We aren't quite sure how to say no, or we are even fearful of saying no. We don't want to disappoint others. But when we cross our own boundaries and say yes to something that isn't energetically aligned in that moment, we end up disappointing others or, perhaps even worse, disappointing ourselves. How often have you gone against your own boundary and said yes to something less than ideal? Not to fret, we've all been there, and I'm here to tell you that you can stop beating yourself up! I want to give you support as you're learning how to say no to *yourself.* Here are two questions that I believe are powerful enough to hinder you from crossing your own boundary:

1. How will I feel if I overstep my own boundary? Will I be upset, disappointed, or angry with myself?
2. How will I feel if I stand firm on my own boundaries? Will I feel empowered and proud of my efforts?

Often it isn't some groundbreaking exercise that will change your behavior—it's the simple shifts that will produce the greatest change. When you walk away from a situation feeling crappy, you are empowered to never have that same outcome again. When you walk away from a situation feeling great, you are empowered to replicate whatever you did so that you can have a similar outcome in the future. It's as simple as that.

So remember, in order to begin feeling more in control of our best yesses, first, we must stand firm on what it is that we want and set boundaries with *ourselves.* Then we must move on to setting them with others.

Setting boundaries with others is important but not easy. So many women ask me for tips on how they can do it all. First, I explain that there is no such thing as doing it all. No one can do every single thing asked of them. But this is where boundaries come in. I have a two-second strategy I teach my clients that helps them set boundaries and create more time to do the things that light them up. This strategy is simply saying the letters *N* and *O* together. This is also exactly what I use on a daily basis. Saying no was something foreign to me for most of my life. For years I was a people pleaser. I loved saying yes. I loved how it made me feel important. I loved the validation it gave me when I had access to all of these opportunities. But ladies, I did nothing with excellence. I was tired, spread way too thin, and resentful, and I eventually began losing out on opportunities that would have been ideal had I not been burned out.

How did I actually start saying no to all the less-than-ideal things and yes to what lit me up? I began *setting boundaries with the day-to-day encounters*. It started with emails and message requests. I bided my time by first saying, "Let me get back to you." It's important that when you are presented with something that is clearly an automatic no, say no. But if you really aren't sure, set a boundary with yourself that you won't decide until you've given yourself some thinking time. We live in this age where we get a text message, a DM, a PM, or an email and we think we need to get that person an answer right away. Whoever made up this silly idea? Just because people are more accessible through technology doesn't mean our decision-making capabilities need to become supercharged as well. I get tons of emails from people pitching collaborations or requesting to be on my podcast. My rule to myself is to never answer right away unless I know 100 percent that it's a no.

Oftentimes we find ourselves having a super-hectic day, with all the emails rolling in at once, and we're in a place of an overwhelmed, *Leave me alone, I don't want to see one more email today* state of mind. Tell me I'm not the only one who has wanted to throw my phone out the window if one more email arrived?! You get the picture. Usually you are not in the best mindset to make a decision in the middle of a hectic day. You'll often be pulled to say yes not because you're interested, but because you're overwhelmed, feel put on the spot, and haven't had space to think. In this moment, I take space, give myself twelve to twenty-four hours, and then evaluate first thing the next morning before my inbox begins filling up yet again. This allows me to make a decision from a place of empowerment rather than pressure. If you can live by this, your yesses will always be best yesses.

I also frequently use the phrase, "Let me check my calendar." Whether someone asks me to review their product, requests a business collaboration, or wants to grab lunch to get my opinion on something, I always give it a little time. Again, when you find yourself being bombarded by all the questions at once, it's easy to make a decision from a place of pressure. When you tell the other person that you acknowledge their request *and* you need some time to look at your calendar, it sets a boundary that (1) indicates that it's not an immediate yes and that they may need to find a backup, and (2) enables you to make a decision that's not rushed. When I use this technique before responding with a definite answer, when I get back to them, they often say that they already found someone else. And in these cases, it makes my decision that much easier!

When opportunities come your way, do you typically feel pressured to give the answer right away? If so, how would it feel to be able to confidently say, "Let me get back to you?" If you had put this new tactic into practice in your life and business, how many things in the last six weeks would you have actually said no to? Ladies, this one has been a *complete* game changer for me, and I believe it will be for you.

In all boundary setting, it's important to separate your big yesses from your smaller yesses. Not all boundaries are going to be life altering, but they will bring about more simple, in-the-moment effects. We know that practicing our best yesses in the small things will yield an easier experience giving our best yesses in the big things. If you can begin saying no to all those little things you once would have reluctantly agreed to, you will have exponentially more space available when the big opportunities come your way. And when those possibilities arise, I highly suggest you take an even more strategic approach by setting aside time to check in with your gut.

Listening to That Gut Feeling

Since we've discussed how to handle decision making through strategy, I think it's about time we dive into how we can use our intuition in this process. I wish that listening to your gut was a clear step-by-step process that I could offer you, but unfortunately, it isn't that simple to navigate. I'm sure you've been at a crossroads before with a big opportunity in front of you. It can feel debilitating, even paralyzing. It would be ideal if you could just think, meditate, or journal and the plan would be clear, but more times than not, it takes some nurturing and practice.

When we are *in* something, we often want to know the *why* right away. So when I was offered what I thought was my dream to join as an affiliate for Marie Forleo's B-School, why was I sensing it wasn't the right timing? Why did I feel pulled to say no to something that I wanted? Ladies, there is usually a reason. We don't always see it immediately, but usually it becomes clear with time. Within weeks of B-School launching, I found out I was pregnant again (my first was just nine months at that time!). Not only was I going to be birthing a baby, but I also was about to birth this book. By saying not yet to B-School, I had left space and bandwidth for my current season of life. If I had acted on that special launch opportunity because of a fear of missing out, it wouldn't have been a great thing. This allowed me to fully enjoy the wondrous things in that current life season, and who knows, maybe I'll still become a B-School affiliate in the future.

How did I have the confidence to say no? Here are some tangible takeaways and tips when you're seeking clarity and discernment:

- Keep this affirmation in your back pocket: I trust that I'll have the discernment to make a confident and aligned decision.
- Talk to people who know you for accountability.
- Do your pros and cons list. You can snag this worksheet back in Lie #2.
- Give yourself time and space—time to mull it over and space to think about other things so it's not all-consuming. Make sure that you don't overload yourself with noise so that you can *honor* the time and space.
- Remind yourself that even if you make the "wrong" decision (never a wrong one, just a not-as-right one!), you will never be too far in to make the decision to back out. This always takes a huge amount of pressure off.

- Finally, get quiet with yourself and imagine the outcome. If you were to say yes, would you have a pit of
  doubt in your stomach? If you were to say no, would
  you have a pit of doubt in your stomach? This was
  probably the step that brought the most clarity in my
  situation.

Are you at a crossroads today and unsure of whether you
should say yes or walk away from an opportunity? I urge you
to take some time and review my last six points. Give yourself
space to process and journal your thoughts. Really listen to
what you feel your gut is saying. I assure you that if you follow
these steps you will never make a wrong decision, but I want
you to be free to pursue the opportunities that are beautifully
aligned for you and your life. The more often you say no to
the mediocre, the more space you have for wondrous blessings in your life.

LIE #7

I Can't Possibly Have a Successful Business *and* Be a Good Mom

I *can barely handle myself, my business, and my current respon-*
sibilities. How will I ever be able to handle another human
being who is dependent on me?

This was the limiting belief that plagued me for years.
Motherhood felt so foreign and frightening, I couldn't imagine
being able to handle a business and motherhood successfully.
After being married for four years and with my husband for
sixteen, people started asking us all the time when we were
going to start a family. And each year as I got older and more
immersed in entrepreneurship, I was no longer convinced that
I actually wanted children. I would tell people, "We'll see. I'll
decide when I'm thirty-five. For now I'm more than happy
with Turbo, our rescue pup, and maybe adopting a few more
pups along the way."

It wasn't that I didn't want kids. It was that I didn't know if kids would want me. Who would want a mom who worked 24/7 and didn't have time to watch them grow and develop? I was so stuck in my head—trapped by my own limited thinking—that I believed there were two choices in life: career success without kids or having kids and placing career on the back burner indefinitely. Again, it wasn't that I didn't want to be a mom, but I couldn't imagine my life having meaning without my business. Does this ring true for any of you?

Flipping the Script

In July of 2016, I received a phone call that would radically transform my outlook on family. Up until this point, as I've said, I had decided to put even the thought of having a family on hold. I was much too busy with my business. After all, I truly believed I was reaching those levels of monetary success I'd been promised by the shiny world of online entrepreneurship. I had finally figured out the formula—work harder, work faster, go big or go home. And I had a choice, as I saw it: I could stay on this fast ride to building my empire (and, although I couldn't see it then, burning out), or I could essentially die a lot inside and have a mediocre, boring life with regular business hours and a family. My pride wanted the first. I had worked so hard to build this momentum. I was just about to close my first $18,000 month, and if I could keep it up, this number could be my new monthly normal.

That fall I planned to attend a business retreat in Colorado. This was something I knew I needed. I told myself that I would work hard from spring until then so I could "earn" this weekend off to just focus on the business and myself. It sounds crazy now—Easter until the end of September to work as hard as possible to earn this time off? But I wasn't about to last that long, and my life was about to get shaken up in a big way.

Each participant of the retreat was given a "camp counselor"—one of the retreat leaders or workshop facilitators—ahead of time to connect with. I had hoped that I would be paired with someone who could give me a little nugget of business strategy to help expedite my success before the retreat. Instead, when I was given her name I discovered that she was set to present on topics that all related to family and work-life balance. (I found this out after doing a little Instagram stalking.) Eek—was she going to ask me if I wanted a family? What was she going to think when I told her I didn't want to talk about it? All sorts of dread and shame filled my mind as I dialed her number.

But the kind, warm voice on the other end of the line put me immediately at ease. "So happy to connect, Kate!" I waited for her to ask me when I would be having babies and creating more work-life balance, but it didn't quite go that way (thank God!). Instead, I shared with her about how great my business was doing; yet, I admitted, my life was crazy and I felt I was about to crash. Strangely, as I opened up to her about the stress I was feeling, I began to feel at peace. She listened quietly and eventually asked, "What about family and having kids? Is that something you want?" I'd been expecting to get worked up and defensive. But I didn't. I told her how I felt about kids, and she lovingly listened, reflecting back to me my hopes and desires.

I walked away from that call feeling different. I had lightness about my future, and I even had lightness in my heart about becoming a mother. Let's not get too far ahead of ourselves though! I had a lightness about becoming a mother *in the future*—you know, once I reached a "next level" where I would be better equipped mentally, financially, and emotionally to handle motherhood. Anyone else relate? Possibly someday, I told myself, but no way right now.

Even so, my husband and I began to talk more about it. I felt my heart shifting for some unknown reason at the time. I began to believe that maybe I could do both—it didn't have to be an either/or situation. Within weeks I started saying things like, "I could see myself becoming pregnant in a year or so." Then that next week my period was a day late, then three, then five, then seven, then ten. Holy guacamole, I was not ready for this! A sea of emotions flooded through my mind. *Yes, I opened up to her about possible dreams outside of work, but that didn't mean I was ready to be a mom today.* So I reluctantly took the pregnancy test, shaking in my boots. Mind you, ladies, I was thirty years old, married, had an income, a house, a dog, and family close by. It wasn't like I was a struggling teenager, but I was still scared.

I opened my eyes. Negative. Not pregnant.

Then something happened I never expected—I felt sad.

I felt really sad. I realized something within me really wanted that test to be positive. I also felt confused, because two weeks prior I wasn't even sure if I'd ever want to be a mother. But in that moment, the maternal instinct entered. For whatever reason, I had experienced that "scare," and it opened up the beautiful realization that I could become a mother and maybe it would all be okay; I could be an entrepreneur too.

Over the next month I felt quite low. I started to worry there was something wrong with me. I started shaming myself for my past eating disorder. Why would a perfectly healthy woman not get a period? The obvious answer is stress, but I went down a dark path of shame and blame. I began believing that because of how I'd treated my body in the past, I would not be able to have children. I must have damaged something, or maybe I just wasn't supposed to have kids and pass my issues on to them. Ladies, this is irrational and I hate saying it all out loud, but I want you to know that if you've dealt with shame around the areas of getting pregnant or having kids, you're not alone. Our minds can use shame effectively in this arena, and we have to be on guard to fight against it.

Flash forward to one month later. I had buried myself in my work, and the last three weeks had been the most productive I'd had in a *long* time. Throwing myself into the work had also helped quiet those fears and kept me busy. Although my mind was occupied with work, however, I began to notice feeling rather emotional. Maybe I was PMSing? But something just felt different. Oh man. No way. There was no way I could possibly be pregnant, was there? I ran to the closet and grabbed the box of pregnancy tests. I took one. I knew it even before I looked.

I was pregnant.

I was pregnant and having a girl. I was pregnant, I was having a girl, and my baby girl was coming early. I can't tell you how I knew all of this, but I felt it deep within my soul. I had a sense that it was all going to be okay.

All three tests that day were positive. I was surprisingly elated. I felt this was terrible timing, but I also felt this was the best timing.

The Many Lies

This experience broke through the first, most basic lie I believed about motherhood and business: that I couldn't do it.

I was gifted with a child and also gifted with the ability to rise to the challenge. But that doesn't mean that I didn't confront many other false beliefs along the way—and continue to confront them today. There are so many lies that surround this complex topic of motherhood and business, many of which you may experience on a daily basis.

Motherhood is messy, and motherhood is complicated. Unfortunately, though, we too often believe that there is a "right way"—which leaves us burdened by feelings of guilt or inadequacy. And there are no right or wrong ways of approaching it. From this mess of mom guilt dozens of lies arise—lies that prevent us from living in or experiencing our full potential. I could fill an entire book solely with the lies that we believe about business and motherhood, but in order to keep you moving along, I am going to stick with a few of the most pressing ones I've encountered as both a mother and a business coach. They include:

- If motherhood doesn't look a certain way, I must be failing (a.k.a. comparisonitis).
- I am a failure if I ask for help.
- If I don't have kids, I'm lacking somehow as a woman.
- My business isn't ready for me to be a mom.

Now let's break these down a bit.

If Motherhood Doesn't Look a Certain Way, I Must Be Failing

I wish I could say I was the new mom who loved every minute of her baby's infancy while keeping the house in order, running the business, and inviting friends and family over for tea and dessert. I wish I could say I had the perfect Instagram-worthy pictures of baby and me wearing one of those postbirth matching floral robe and swaddle sets. I really wish I could say that I wanted to join a moms group and hear the lowdown on the baby-led weaning craze. But this is the furthest thing from the truth.

In reality, my life looked nothing like that. I avoided people. I cried over everything and anything. I was frustrated that other people didn't seem to understand why I couldn't deal with them popping over to the house unannounced just to say hi. I felt so alone and even angry with everyone. This was not fun, and this was not how I'd envisioned motherhood. My plan had backfired. Why hadn't anyone told me babies don't ever sleep? Oh wait, they did tell me, and I ignored their remarks my entire pregnancy. #Winning. #MomOfTheYear. Not only did I feel like a failure for not listening to the baby warnings, but in addition, I felt like a failure in my business, marriage, and relationships.

This work-life balance thing wasn't working. In fact, there were several times when I came close to throwing in the towel on the business altogether. And I can remember one day quite vividly. Baby Annabelle still would not take a bottle, and I was a frazzled mess. She wasn't sleeping. I wasn't sleeping. No showering. No hair brushing (I lived on dry shampoo). As the nanny we had at the time struggled to get Annabelle to take her bottle, I found myself on the couch, hooked up to the breast pump (before I knew about the portable ones) as I listened to the lawn guys starting their mowers. I bet you can imagine what came next—the noise set off my ninety-seven-pound pup, Turbo, which sent him running to the window and

121

simultaneously tripping over my breast pump cords, yanking the suction cups right off of me.

Ouch! And there goes the milk I so painstakingly pumped. That was painful and messy—a metaphor of what my life was like in that moment: pure chaos.

I felt like a complete failure each and every time I signed onto social media and saw those moms who were just "doin' it all." I could barely do one thing well, much less all of it. A lie was worming its way into my heart: *You're not as good at this mom thing as everyone else.* At its root, the lie was based on one thing—comparison. I was comparing myself to every other female businesswoman out there and thinking, *How does she make it look so easy? Why can't I do it like that? What's wrong with me?*

Comparison is a subtly destructive force and in stark contrast to another ten-letter *c*-word: *confidence*. I love putting these two words side by side because they serve as a reminder that when we compare, when we belittle ourselves and desire the lives of others, it eats away at our own confidence. We buy into the lie that we aren't good enough or capable enough— and we start to live from a place of discontentment. And in doing so, we rob our hearts of the joy that we can have today.

It can be so tempting to compare yourself to other moms out there; to compare your choice to send your littles to daycare so that you can work in a peaceful environment to the moms Instagramming all their perfect homeschool outings; to compare yourself to the moms whose babies sleep all day and who can still shower, wear real jeans, and put on makeup; and even to compare yourself to yourself. Yep, you read that correctly. We constantly compare our today selves to our past selves. Your pre-pregnancy weight. Your pre-baby energy. The copious amount of time you once had and today have no idea what you spent it on and would do anything to have it back. I'm asking you today to STOP comparing yourself in any of these categories. It will only leave you frustrated and racked with guilt, anxiety, and even anger.

Breaking the habit of comparison is easier said than done. How can you put an end to the lie of comparison that threatens to zap you of joy and confidence? Something that has been instrumental for my clients is creating personal love notes (affirmations). Here are some examples I have heard that may help you:

- I can let it all go and be okay.
- I can surrender AGAIN and still be strong.
- It's okay if it takes forever to get comfortable with being uncomfortable.
- I can't compare my monetary success TODAY to my monetary success a year ago.
- I must give myself permission and grace to ONLY do what I have the strength to do.

I challenge you today to write out your own list of love notes in the space below to use when comparison and fears begin creeping in:

_____

_____

_____

_____

_____

Here is another one for you: when comparisonitis strikes, tell yourself, *I'm a good mom because I care*; a good friend once told me this, and it honestly was a game changer. Repeat: *If I care, this means that I am doing the very best that I can do.* Especially if you are reading this book, you are likely an overachiever and undercelebrator. You spend more time looking at the things you haven't done right than celebrating that you're keeping your family alive, fed, clothed, and on their way to daycare.

I Have to Do It All Myself; Asking for Help Is Failing

I remember it being a huge hit to my ego seeing the business bring in next to nothing once I had the baby and could no longer work. Before I found out I was pregnant, I had reached my most profitable months yet. It felt impossible to ever get back to those large-number months to help contribute to my family expenses. Annabelle was my first baby, and I didn't know what I was doing. I felt like I was making mistakes left and right. People offered to help, but I felt like a burden. I remembered how chaotic my life was before a baby, which made me assume theirs was probably just as busy. I decided it was easier to try doing it on my own than to live with the guilt of burdening others.

Well, that insistence on doing things myself almost resulted in the death of my business. As we drove back from a Fourth of July family barbecue, something in my overworked, overstressed self snapped and I began bawling my eyes out in the car, telling my husband I just couldn't deal with it all anymore. I was convinced I had failed at motherhood *and* business. I wasn't doing either of them well, and I couldn't walk away from my mama title, so I needed to walk away from the business. My husband tried talking me out of it and, hoping to be helpful, suggested we sign the baby up for daycare. It was a reasonable suggestion—but for me, it triggered even more insecurity and failure. My daughter will now need to be cared for by someone else because her mother is incapable of doing it herself! I began to sob harder. Anyone else engage in this lie before? However untrue it may be, it can feel absolutely *brutal*!

Rationally we all know that believing we're a failure because we have to ask for help is a lie. Many children are raised in childcare or watched over by family members because most individuals don't have work-from-home businesses that allow for flexibility. You aren't a failure if you decide that you need to earn an income and have someone else watch your child as you do so. You aren't a failure if you decide that four hands are better than two, and that you need someone to come in and help with the heavy load of being a working mom. As I'm sure you've heard before, it takes a village to raise a child!

I had bought into the lie that daycare somehow meant I wasn't a good mom, but as I wrestled with the idea, something switched. I thought, *I already feel like a failure, spread so thin with the baby home with me, I actually think I could be a better mom if I could quickly set aside this ego and decide to ask for help*. As I said this out loud and talked it over with my husband, it began to logically and emotionally make more sense for me.

Shortly after surrendering control and admitting we needed childcare, I felt complete peace. I handed the heavy lifting over to people who could help and no longer carried it myself. My goal was to be the best mama that I could be, and in time, motherhood began to feel different. I was more present for my baby, and I had a peace within myself that I was going to be okay financially and, more important, emotionally.

As I asked for help with Annabelle, I began to realize that I also needed to ask for help in my business. As much as I wanted to do everything myself, I couldn't. But I had to lay my ego down to take the first steps and begin to reach out. So I ended up hiring more support onto my team to work the back end of my business—and it was the best decision I could have made. They became the glue that holds everything together and the reason I'm still operating today. They picked up the pieces that I had dropped and did what I was no longer capable of doing. I let go of control when I couldn't do the heavy lifting myself, and I replaced it with women who were eager to work alongside me to care for my business and baby in a beautiful way.

The lie of having to do it all is powerful. We often resist asking for help, believing it to be a sign of weakness when in truth it is simply a way to step into freedom and become stronger in every area of life. But how can we defeat it? Here are three tangible ways to step into freedom:

1. Drop the guilt. When you need help simply *ask for it.* You are not the first to mother, nor the first to feel the guilt. I have yet to hear of a woman who did it all herself. So lean on those who offer (guilt free)! I used to feel bad even when people offered to help because I felt like I was inconveniencing them. With time, I've learned to trust that those who offer are honest and

boundaried enough to tell me when they aren't available. What also helps me drop the guilt is realizing that even though I may not find it a joy to care for a screaming toddler, some ladies (often it's my kid-less friends) actually don't mind! They've voiced that they enjoy it. So remember, you allowing others to take a load off your back may be the exact thing that they are looking for.

2. Be willing to pay. Hire the right support within your business depending on the season you are in. Yes, this means letting go of some control and increasing your overhead costs—but there will be seasons in your business when this is essential. And you've got to do so *before* you are in a panic or before your business begins to fall apart because you're trying to do too much. As I began to outsource tasks and roles in my business, I found it to be really uncomfortable. I wondered how I would pay employees and if it would be worth it. But in time, I began to see the return on my investment and, most important, my sanity.

3. Be willing to give to get. One way to find more freedom in your business is to link arms with others. I hear many women say they can't afford childcare, and this is where the creative thinking cap must go on. How can you link arms to find what it is that you need? Is there another mom on the block who can swap a few hours with you each week? You watch her kids with yours for a few hours and she watches yours the next day. Or is there a high school student studying child development and looking for experience that

you can pay a few bucks to play with the kids while you get some work in? These are just two examples, but there are many creative ways we receive help by giving help.

If I Don't Have Kids, I Am Lacking Somehow as a Woman

This insidious lie works its way into our minds from a very early age—and it can eat us alive if we're not careful. Although we are all mothers in some way, traditional motherhood is not for everyone—and it's essential to be able to claim this truth for yourself. When I say "traditional motherhood," I mean consciously making the decision to raise a child whether biological, fostered, or adopted.

I truly believe we are called to represent different roles in mamahood. You may adore kids but know you want the kind you can return to their parents after feeding them copious amounts of sugar, spoiling them with cartoons past their bedtime, and buying them a new litter of French bulldogs. You play a huge role in the lives of these children and help their parents be better moms and dads themselves by presenting them with some time alone for an evening. Some of you have also decided to mother adults. You open your homes to college students to uplift and encourage them, you serve at soup kitchens, you visit those who are sick and send meals. You selflessly give your time to serve those in need.

Ladies, mothering looks so different for each of us, but when it comes down to it, *each* of us can nurture and embody motherhood in some way. And it's important to accept that the mothering season you are in is the right one for you. For those who are trying to start families but are unable to,

I can't imagine your pain and frustration, but just know you *are* a mother in this season. For those of you experiencing the grueling process of waiting for your sweet adoptive babies, I can't imagine the hardship, but remember, you *are* a mother in this season. For the woman who is caring for a sick relative and feels like her life is on hold, I commend you and am sending you a warm blanket of love while you *are* a mother in this season. You can nurture even when that looks different from what you envisioned. The underlying truth doesn't change that you *are* a mother in this season.

Each time you begin doubting your decision to remain childless or feel frustration around the timing of becoming a mother, stop in your tracks and repeat this: "I am a mother exactly where I am today."

Then ask yourself, *What can I do to help fulfill this role within me right now?* Is it adopting a fur baby? Is it volunteering at the assisted living home down the street? Is it taking in a friend who recently lost her job and found herself in a financial crisis? Is it making a meal for the woman in your book club who just started chemo?

Bottom line: You are important. Exactly where you are.

My Business Isn't Ready for Me to Be a Mom

Ah, the lie of readiness (Lie #2, anyone?). Whether it's worry that you're not financially ready, not mature enough, don't have enough time, don't have the skills to be a good mom— here's the truth: you are more than ready and equipped to be a mama and at the same time never prepared enough. Those of you who are scared and afraid today, wondering whether you are ready and capable of becoming a mother, just know—you will never be ready enough, and you *are* capable of being a mother and running a business. Be confident that whatever motherhood looks like for you, it is possible to pair it with a business and to do so successfully.

Motherhood was exactly what my business needed. I went from working sixteen-hour days to my current sixteen-hour weeks. I was on the verge of losing everything due to the path I had laid for myself. And today, not only do I have a thriving business making an even bigger income and impact than I was during those long work days, but I have two babes under the age of two, a loving relationship with my husband, an intentional social life, and I don't feel like my life is one step from imploding. The snapshot you'll see of me today I never once believed I would be capable of handling. And if I had waited until I was ready and could reduce my work hours, I honestly would still be waiting.

I chuckle as I write this because now that I am a mama I totally get it. Motherhood is what prepared me for motherhood. I don't think we are ever 100 percent ready to try something new. Do you agree? I want to challenge you to think of the things you once felt unprepared for and how that turned out for you. I bet you handled it better than you anticipated. I bet those fears you replayed for so long never actually came to fruition. It's funny how we spend so many hours playing scenarios in our minds that never actually happen. We vent with others about how these circumstances could ruin our life and the path we have planned. What if we just took half of that worry time about not feeling ready or qualified enough, surrendered it, and believed that somewhere deep within, we were gifted with the power to make this possible? I know it isn't always easy to believe this truth. I get it, ladies: when we are in what I call the swirl, our minds race, panic, and replay old failures and potential future failures. So how can we defeat this lie that we aren't ready or capable?

First, give yourself some space to process, pray, or meditate on the emotions you're experiencing around readiness and capability.

Then, lay out the real evidence of what is going on. Don't let your thoughts spin out of control and trap you in lies. Work through the voice you're hearing and combat it with facts surrounding the situation.

Finally, sit down and do a quick five-minute mindset exercise to reorient your mind. Here's how it works:

Grab a pen and paper. Now ask yourself, *In the last year, what have I actually started or accomplished that I didn't feel ready for? In the last five years? In the last ten years?*

My guess is that you'll fill up the page. You'll be shocked to find that anything of value in your life you began before you were ready. No one is ever fully ready to become a mother. Repeat after me: "I can have a successful business and be a good mom. If I am capable of loving others, I am ready to be a mom. And, because I actually care about being ready enough to be a good mom, this makes me a good mom."

You Made It

No matter where you are today, rest assured knowing that you are exactly where you are supposed to be. Whether you relate to how I felt, that you can't be a good business owner and have enough time to be a mama; or if you worry that you won't have enough time to start your business with a family; or if you feel like a failure for sending your kids to daycare; or ultimately you decide that kids aren't your calling—I believe that you are capable of handling the dreams that you have. It doesn't have to be one over the other!

Remember that we are always being prepared for the next season. Each new bump in the road brings about a fresh perspective on life, motherhood, friendship, family, and business. Leaning into this will build resiliency and capability—the very things we need to think like a boss. I know that personally, without my painful, fear-filled season of entering motherhood, this chapter wouldn't exist. How often do we allow our mind to get stuck in the way things "should be happening," believing there is a right way in which our life should be unfolding? There is something even better waiting for us as we continue to move forward, even if it's a little bit messy. Release. Surrender. You just get to show up, hands open, ready to receive that beauty that is waiting for you.

LIE #8

I Need My Friends' and Family's Understanding in Order to Succeed

I t was a cold, sunny December day in Manhattan. Christmas music and the warm smell of chestnuts and hot pretzels filled the air of Rockefeller Center. I was en route to Radio City Music Hall to see the Rockettes with my family to celebrate my dad's birthday. It was exactly one year since I had left my nine-to-five to run my own business full time. Our first stop was Bouchon Bakery to get some warm drinks and sweets. Sounds like a picture-perfect day, right?

Except, it looked a little more like this: I was utterly exhausted from staying up way too late the night before, working on my newly-birthed second business. I was burned out and on the verge of tears. My family was having a jolly good time as we strolled by the shops while I was trailing three feet behind, glued to my phone. *Kate, can't you just put it away for ten minutes?* These words had been said to me in the past, and now they played on repeat in my mind. My feelings of guilt were sky-high, but part of me also churned with resentment. I kept thinking to myself, *You guys don't get it. You don't own an online business, and you don't understand the demands of entrepreneurship.* I wanted to scream. Rather than yearning to be present and in the moment with my family, I felt angry, frustrated, and misunderstood. Most of all, I wanted to leave so that I could get work done. This was the day I began building walls around nonentrepreneurial people in my life.

Before becoming an entrepreneur, business owners close to me would voice similar feelings, and I always thought I was helping by offering my two cents. When I noticed entrepreneurial friends working around the clock, I jumped in and lovingly encouraged them to turn off, set better boundaries, hire an assistant, or even get more organized. I couldn't comprehend how they could be so powerless over their time when, in fact, they were their own boss. Didn't people leave the corporate world so they could create margin and no longer answer to a boss? I used to think they were doing it to themselves for some odd reason. I began noticing that if I said anything to help, they became defensive, frustrated, and eventually closed themselves off from discussing business around me.

Through that experience and then the insight I gained as a business owner myself, I learned two things, both of which we will dive into in this chapter. First, no one but you can fully understand (or cares to understand) the demands of your business, and this is true for anything in life. There is no one but you who can fully comprehend what you're going through. This is true whether it's your business, your health, the loss of a relationship or loved one, financial issues, or any other area of your life. Others can show empathy and compassion for what you are facing, but no one has walked in your shoes. And second, I learned that you *don't need* anyone to fully understand your circumstances in order to be successful. You may think the friend who worked for a small local business would get the hustle and what it's like to be "on" 24/7, but maybe they don't. You can be successful even without understanding or validation from others.

We all want to be seen, heard, and understood by those around us. But when it comes right down to it, no one in your life will truly understand what your business requires except for you, and that's okay. This may sound lonely or discouraging, but it doesn't have to be. In fact, leaning into the fact that others can't fully understand your entrepreneurial path—and that they don't have to—can help you experience freedom for yourself and grace toward others, something that will benefit all of you.

Why We Think We Need Our Friends and Family to Get It

Has feeling misunderstood by those in your life been a struggle for you in your business journey? How have you allowed the desire to be understood to rule over your business and take control of your dream? Getting stuck on the lie that we need our friends and family to understand and support all aspects of our business can be crippling. I see it in a myriad of ways with the women I coach, often starting from our first sales call together. Many will say, "I really want to join this program, but my significant other isn't fully supportive of my business. He just doesn't get it, and I need him to understand in order to feel good about my decision and move forward."

Can you relate? Do you ever feel like no one quite understands your dream the way that you do and that they must
completely understand in order for you to succeed? In your
mind it's as clear as day, but you can't always find the words to
articulate the vision to others around you. And because of this,
your dream is stifled—you've bought into the lie that if others
don't understand, you can't move forward. And as you carry
this belief around, your reality will come to mirror it. Clients
who say they can't move forward until their significant other
understands them are usually the ones who end up putting
their success on the back burner. They decide to sit and wait
for the day to come when their partner may just possibly begin
to understand their vision. Sometimes this day doesn't arrive.

Though the belief that we need others to understand our
dreams and visions can be deeply embedded in our mind, the
reason for this limited thinking is actually fairly simple. It
goes back to cognitive distortions, particularly self-fulfilling
prophecies. What we believe, we see. If we run our businesses
telling ourselves no one fully understands and we can't be
successful unless they do, this will be true—our success will
be dependent on others, we will wait forever for them to fully
understand, and we will often feel resentful. On the other
hand, if we tell ourselves that others don't have to fully understand our vision in order for us to reach success, we will begin
to take the pressure off those relationships and feel less stifled,
more supported, and capable of experiencing success.

And yet, if we're aware of the issue and see that the solu-
tion is straightforward and simple, why do we continue to
hold on to this mentality? The fact is, for most of us, this lie
has become all-consuming, and we can't even recognize when
it's manifesting and derailing our success. I believe this is a

protective mechanism. Rather than risking disappointment, we accept disappointment even before it's manifested. We think there is less risk of being hurt if we first assume we'll be hurt. It really boils down to having zero expectations: if we tell ourselves we will probably fail at business, then we won't be disappointed when we do. The trouble is that by setting our expectations low, we actually increase the chance of failing because we aren't even reaching for the higher rung. If we tell ourselves we will never earn enough income for our spouse to retire, we won't have to be disappointed when we don't earn enough income for our spouse to retire. And the same goes for trying to get others to understand our grand vision. Often we don't even try, because it feels like the safer option. We tell ourselves, *They will never get it*, and we don't have to feel disappointed when this comes true. But is this really what you want? Do you want to go through life expecting that your friends and family just won't get it and telling yourself that you can't succeed because of them?

I want you to repeat after me: "No one will believe in my dreams to the extent that I do—and I don't need them to in order to be successful."

It's important to recognize that as much as your significant other loves and cares for you, they may not fully understand your dreams. The same is true of your family and friends. If you can accept this early on and let go of needing others to validate what you're doing, you will find so much more fulfillment in the mission you are striving for. You can practice confidence in *not* needing others' words or approval for you to feel good about your business or your worth. You can find your strength in championing and working toward your own dreams.

Adjusting Our Outlook

Once we've accepted that our friends and family may not ever fully understand our dream and vision, and that we don't *need* them to in order to succeed, how can we experience more peace? Let's dive into some practical tips that will help adjust our mindset in this area.

Shift Your Thinking and Be Open for Discussion

Ever hear the phrase, "It's not them, it's you"? This one always hits a nerve for me. When I first began therapy in my twenties, my therapist suggested that in order for me to begin feeling more understood by friends and family, I needed to adjust my behaviors. Oh, I bet you can imagine how fun this was to hear. However, she was right. So rather than react defensively when people offended me, I took her advice and started to breathe, step back, and pause before reacting.

So today I'm challenging you to let go of the need to over-explain yourself. When someone utters a remark that leaves you feeling insecure, misunderstood, or dismissed, try this: stop, breathe, and take a moment to reframe what they said. Here are two examples of how to advocate for yourself and be open to conversation.

Example 1

Friend/family member comment: "It must be so nice that you get to play on your phone all day for your business." (My blood is already boiling as I write this example out because I hear it often!)

How you can shift your thinking: First, BREATHE. Step back. Pause. Keep in mind that they have NO idea what it is you do for work, just as you had no idea prior to becoming an entrepreneur.

Your response: "I agree! It is really nice that I can work from my phone, although it can be tough at times because I never get to fully unplug like I did when I had a nine-to-five."

Example 2

Friend/family member comment: "I should just become an entrepreneur. It seems so easy to work on your couch and earn a living."

How you can shift your thinking: Again, BREATHE. Step back. Pause.

Your response: "It is definitely nice getting to create an income by working from my couch. Before becoming an entrepreneur I also thought it looked easy or glamorous, but little did I know how much work and sacrifice it would require even for a little bit of success."

Remember, this is about educating others and advocating for yourself rather than overexplaining. Yes, there is a subtle difference. Advocating is stating the facts without explanation. You can reframe what was said, state the facts (educate) in a nondefensive way, be open for conversation, and then move on.

You may begin to see that a nondefensive and unattached effort to educate those around you creates more understanding. So many of you have voiced that it just feels easier to accept that others will not understand and live defensively rather than trying to create awareness. You can carry resentment that others don't understand, or you can join in the work of helping to reframe the conversation and share more about the reality of being a business owner. If you make this change, I think you'll be pleasantly surprised at the results!

Know When to Stop Trying and Lean into Acceptance

If you've attempted to educate your loved ones and there is no change or movement, it's time to practice acceptance. Many loved ones want to better understand what you are going through and will do the necessary work to get there. However, for some reason or another, others may not be able or willing to do this. It doesn't mean that they don't care about you. They may not be in a place to offer understanding and support in the way that you'd like. In these instances, my honest advice is to quit trying. It isn't worth pouring your heart and energy into a conversation about something the other person doesn't value as much as you do. You know those friends with whom you just can't talk politics, but you still love them and find other things to talk about? This is similar. You may find that there are some loved ones you just don't talk business with. This doesn't mean that it'll always be that way, but it means that you are not pouring energy into something that feels like a lost cause—energy that could be better spent on building your business and achieving the goals that truly matter to you.

I've been there before. I tried educating a certain someone about my business and felt more and more rejected with every attempt. I decided to stop caring about their approval or trying to elicit their support. To my surprise, something eventually shifted and the individual, of their own accord, became interested in knowing more and supporting me in my business. I was completely shocked. I even teared up when this person went out of their way to help me on a project in my business.

I had never expected that they would be the one to reach out. And it reminded me that when we release and surrender control, we are often blessed with something unexpected.

Give Yourself the Validation That You Most Need

I said it earlier in the chapter, but let me reiterate it here: your view of success cannot hinge on the approval of others. You do not need other people to believe in your work the way you do. What's most important is that YOU see it. During my time in business I have learned to *first* find validation within. With the opinions of others being so readily available via social media these days, I notice many people seeking validation before starting a project, and it can go wrong. Yes, polling people and getting feedback can be helpful in business—when the entire audience is your ideal customer. But the people who follow your business on social media or through your email newsletter are likely not all ideal customers. One may be your best friend, who is invested in your success, one may be your dear aunt Sally, and so on. Getting everyone and their mother's opinion (quite literally) can be a detriment to your success. This is why it's so important that you check in with YOU and ask: *What is it that I want or believe will work?*

Bye-Bye, External Validation

It is important to become mindful of the times you find yourself slipping into the pattern of needing external validation. You may see this happening in the midst of change or up-leveling in your business, when you are stepping out of your comfort zone. You may become hypersensitive and begin to

141

doubt your decisions, turning to others to validate or approve of your choices. This can lead to an excessive need for external validation rather than trusting your intuition and knowledge. Recently a client was struggling with this when she was about to raise her prices. Uncertain of the decision, she began seeking approval from friends and family—and found herself getting all kinds of different opinions, which only threw her deeper into confusion and uncertainty. Over a few sessions we worked together to help her believe in herself in spite of outside opinions. In the end she was able to move forward, satisfied with her decision to charge more, without needing approval from others.

How often do you need to hear from others that your idea is valid or you're doing a good job? Reflect on this question as you think about the past day, week, and month. Are you hindered by your need to receive external approval? Again— and I say this gently, because I've been there—if you need outside affirmation to feel fulfilled, you are setting yourself up for disappointment. Our fulfillment should come from a deep-rooted confidence in ourselves.

Here are a few mantras for when you find yourself relying too heavily on outside approval:

- My worth is not dependent on others' opinions.
- I am confident in the work that I do whether others validate it or not.
- I have been placed in this position because I am capable.
- I can take the energy I would be spending on earning others' approval and instead dive headfirst into my mission.

As business owners, it can be easy to fixate on our own shortcomings and issues. Because our business is a direct reflection of us, we can become hyperfocused on people pleasing and image. We often forget that it isn't about us but about serving our clients and customers. I encourage you for the next month to become more aware of how often you allow others' opinions or lack of excitement to trigger you. How much time and mental space is this filling?

With practice, I've learned to let go of what others think of me. I've realized that the ones who are judging are not the ones I am serving. And the ones that I serve need the best of me. I can't possibly give my best if I'm caught up in seeking approval from others. Today I am able to be focused with my time and energy because I no longer allow others' opinions of me to dictate how I view myself. I am able to reach more people, create a bigger impact, earn more income, and in turn, this allows me to donate more time and money to causes outside of my business. This success comes from the fact that I've given strict focus to my mission in spite of the noise around me.

Ladies, if you can cling to each of the four points above, I guarantee you will begin to find comfort. Do you want to make a greater impact on those you serve and beyond? If you can release this old pattern of thinking and welcome in the new, you will see exponential growth in yourself, your business, and the mission you are looking to accomplish in life. Stand firmly in your confidence and your mission. And while you're at it, spread this message to your other entrepreneurial friends who are struggling. We no longer have to be held back waiting for approval from others—we've got this!

LIE #9

I Don't Have Enough Time

We can't take another trip. I just don't have enough time. I am working around the clock trying to build this business, while still working at the mental health agency. I don't know how I can possibly create more time, and I certainly can't just take another vacation." That was my conversation with my husband during the summer of 2014. I was in the foundation-laying stage of my therapy practice while still working full time. I felt completely stretched, and all I could do was fantasize about how simple life would be if I could quit my job and have only one thing to focus on. I would sit and daydream (which in turn was wasting time!) not only about the fulfillment I would feel as a full-time business owner but, most importantly, about the spacious daily routine that I'd someday have.

Here's a little peek at what I believed full-time entrepreneurship would look like: wake up early for coffee and reflection/journaling time, then move on to some personal development reading, answer a few emails, go to the gym, come home and shower, make a smoothie, begin my calls for the day, meet other business friends for lunch, come home and work some more in my business, finish by 4 p.m., and have the remainder of the day for me or family/friend time.

Ladies, I had no idea. Like really, let me repeat, no stinkin' idea. I believed that time was dependent on my environment. Well, fast-forward to the day when I finally did step full-time into my business, and I quickly realized that wasn't the case. Time is dependent on your mindset and behaviors. I had this epiphany shortly after quitting my job to take on the business full time, when I took a look around, paused for a moment, and realized that my life was now even more chaotic than it had ever been. How was this possible? I only had one thing to focus on—the business—and I could barely keep my head above water. Here's a snapshot: I had canceled my gym membership, as it had been months since I had worked out; I was declining invitations to see friends or family or go to any type of social event; and any thought of self-care, devotions, or personal development went completely out the window.

How, I asked myself, did I get to this place? I became an entrepreneur so that I could hustle less, stress less, work less, be more fulfilled in life, and have more time for the people and things I loved most. And now, my life felt like utter chaos. Can any of you relate? Maybe you're in a similar place as I was, feeling the discomfort of trying to balance so many things. Maybe you've built a successful empire, but you've crossed your own personal boundaries and no longer have the freedom that you used to. Maybe you're entering a different season in your personal life, which will affect the amount of time you can devote to your business.

So why do we struggle with these beliefs around not having enough time? I think it stems in part from being taught that time is something we have to master. For example, children are often told some form of, "If you can sit quietly for twenty minutes, you will earn a lollipop." We are often rewarded for making the most of time, doing something faster or more efficiently. Time is also a measure of success: "It should only take you *this long* to complete." We are raised with ideals of what time *should* look like and how it's best used, and in this age of hustle, that usually means wrestling time so that you can cram more into it.

As we talked about earlier in the book, we live in a lack-mindset (or scarcity-mindset) society. This kind of thinking is applied to time constantly: You are running out of time. There is only so much of it. You need to get everything accomplished because you don't want to live with regrets. We are taught there is never enough time, and that when we do find extra pockets of time, we must make the most of it. We hear that if we don't, we are essentially *wasting* time. Imagine what the world would be like if we could adopt an abundance mindset around time. What if we believed that we have *enough* time, and that we don't have to frantically wring each minute from the day—allowing us to dive more deeply and presently into the minutes we do have? If we all adopted this mindset, I guarantee there would be a whole lot less stress in the world, people would be much more generous, and a lot of mistakes could also be prevented. Having a scarcity mindset around time causes more problems than it solves, and this takes extra time to fix.

We often use time as a scapegoat, saying, "If I only had more time, I would do _____." Anyone guilty of these?

- I would launch the blog if I had more time.
- I would start that networking group if I had enough time.
- I would get back on the dating websites if my business didn't take so much time from me.
- I would join a small group and meet new women if I had enough time.
- I would write the book if I had enough time.

I know for a fact that we can all raise our hands for at least one of these. Usually the issue has more to do with avoidance, self-sabotage, insecurity, lack of boundaries, low motivation, and other fears. Feeling that we don't have enough time is the manifestation of limited thinking around accomplishing our dreams. In reality, if something is a priority in our life, we will make the time for it. If we really want something, we will often do whatever it takes to rearrange our schedule to make it happen. I have to remind myself of this all the time. Rather than blaming time for the things I'm not doing, I can stop and assess whether there are underlying issues. I am cognizant to catch myself and state the reality: "It's not that I don't have time for this right now, it's that this isn't a priority for me," or "It's not that I don't have time, I'm just afraid of moving forward." There are some ways to shift your perception that will actually help you take on a more expansive mindset around your time.

Reframe Your Thinking

Do you ever find yourself fixating on not having enough time? Do you find that you're sulking, frustrated, even angry, stuck on the fact that there aren't enough hours in the day? You waste minutes, hours, days lost in this frame of thought, feeling sorry for yourself. I get it—I'm nodding my head and raising my hand to this one. But the hard truth is that feeling sorry for ourselves is not going to get the job done or create more time. We've got to establish firm boundaries with ourselves, set the sulking aside, and begin taking small, imperfect steps to begin to address our mentality toward our time.

What would happen if we replaced worry with another thought process? This will free up mental energy and potentially create space to focus on the things we want to be doing. Don't believe me? I challenge you to try keeping a "Worry Tracker." Here is how to get started:

1. Open a note on your phone or a page in your journal and label it "Worry Tracker." Each time you find yourself worrying about not having adequate time to get something done, record how long you spent fixating on not completing the task before taking action.
2. Once the task is finally accomplished, record how long it took to complete.
3. Add up how much time you spent worrying before you accomplished the task. Compare how much time was spent worrying with how long the task actually took to complete.

Throughout the years, many of my clients who have participated in this challenge have noticed a pattern—the amount of time they *believe* a task will take to accomplish ended up being close to the amount of time they spent worrying about beginning the task. Essentially, rather than wasting the time thinking about starting, they could have just made it happen! This is why setting limits with your mind is crucial. Just imagine the amount of time you would have for yourself if you stopped overanalyzing and just went and did it!

I spent far too long believing that what made people successful in business was time. The more time they committed, the more success they would create. But the belief that time equals success is completely inaccurate—what makes people successful is their mindset. If they believe they can succeed with whatever resources are available, they will make do. We have to *choose* how we view things. We can focus on the lack (of time, of money, of energy), or we can focus on the abundance. When we tell ourselves we don't and won't have enough time for something, this becomes a self-fulfilling prophecy. We start to believe it and to live accordingly. Suddenly we actually *don't* have enough time for it.

But what if you began replacing *I don't have enough time* with *I have more than enough time for the things and people I care about*? By reframing your mindset, you can shift your approach and create time for the things you want in your life. Like the examples I provided, our beliefs around time have very little to do with how much time we actually have. More often, our beliefs about time reveal the fear that lives underneath them. Each time you begin to tell yourself there isn't enough time, ask yourself, *What's really going on here?* When you pose this question to yourself, it opens up awareness around what you may really be avoiding. As you adopt this awareness, you will gradually begin to feel more spaciousness in your schedule.

Let's commit to respecting the T-I-M-E word by shifting our approach. Replace *I don't have time* with the actual underlying fact:

- I would launch the blog if I wasn't so scared.
- I would start that networking group if I could get the courage to pick up the phone.
- I would get back on the dating websites if I could be more organized and boundaried in my business.
- I would write the book if I could work through my fear of being seen.

When you can begin to acknowledge that it's not actually time but a fear or priority issue, you can start taking the necessary steps to dig deeper. And then once you've worked through the fear and shifted your thinking, your time will begin to feel more spacious.

Set Limits around Time

Not setting boundaries will leave you feeling like there is never enough time for the things you want to do. People frequently ask me, "How the heck do you do it all? Run a business, manage income properties, host a podcast, mother babies, keep up with household responsibilities"—though you don't know me well enough if you think this!—"all while showing up each and every day on social media?" I tell them it is only because of the tight boundaries I set.

Let's pause for a moment to review the basic dictionary definition of a boundary. The Google dictionary states that a boundary is "a line that marks the limits of an area."[1] Boundaries are complicated but essential to reclaiming our time and shifting our mindsets. I could literally write an entire book concerning this topic (who knows, maybe someday I will!), but today we are going to just scratch the surface.

Going back to the question of how badly you want it, meaning how willing you are to find the time, I invite you to step into your CEO self. *You* are the boss of your life, your business, your well-being, and certainly your boundaries. You need to approach every situation as that boss babe, whether you feel it or not. Then, step into that CEO role to establish boundaries for your time. When you're trying to decide where to invest your energy, check in with your CEO self and get clear on what she wants for herself, her family, and the business, and then set the boundaries accordingly. If that feels fuzzy or difficult for you, try asking yourself two questions to help with boundary setting:

Is this worth missing out on time with friends and family?

Recently, I began asking myself, *Is this worth missing out on time that I could be spending with my babies?* Each and every time, this question clarifies what I want and makes it a whole lot easier for me to cut out the things that don't make my heart jump for joy. Just as we discussed in Lie #6, we don't need to say yes to #allthethings. We can become confident decision makers, saying no to the things we truly don't have an interest in. When someone asks to pick my brain in exchange for lunch or a cup of coffee, I ask myself, *Is a cup of coffee worth missing out on sixty to ninety minutes of my daughters' lives?* My current answer is no, and I say "current" because boundaries are fluid and ever-changing with the seasons. Ask yourself, right now in this season, *Is it worth the time I will be missing out on* _____ *?*

TIP: Have a resource page on your site or a hidden link that you can send to those who want to pick your brain. This has been a lifesaver for me! It has saved me hours, if not days, of time. I include video interviews, podcast episodes, free master classes, workbooks, blog articles, and more.

Does this advance my business goals in a concrete way?

Some may call me selfish or stingy for not accepting coffee dates from strangers, but quite frankly I would rather spend thirty minutes writing a blog post addressing their questions that can be sent to thousands of women and make a much bigger impact on others and, in turn, my business. See the difference? A coffee date would serve one person and a blog post is a scalable way to potentially reach thousands. I ask myself not only, *Is this worth missing out on precious time spent with my family*, but also, *Is this going to advance my business goals in a concrete way?* If the answer is clearly no, I offer the resource page on my website.

Ladies, you don't owe anyone your time. Your time is yours to keep. Sadly, early on in my business I spent hours accommodating others for those brain-picking sessions. Each time I walked away feeling taken advantage of. But I'm a firm believer that we either win or learn in life. Through these instances, I learned that not everyone will respect my time and that I need to stand firm in my own boundaries and say no to something that will potentially leave me feeling resentful or taken advantage of. Through this experience I began to ask myself this question before saying yes to giving my time: *Is there potential value in this encounter for my business as well?* If the answer was no, I knew my own limitations and responded with a firm no.

Accept Time-Barren Seasons

Now another way to overcome the lie of not having enough time is to learn to accept the season you're in. I truly believe we are all given energy, mind space, and stamina to run our own race. I felt a sense that 2016 would be my season to *run*. I didn't just run, but I sprinted, and sprinted hard. This laid the foundation to follow a nudge in 2017 to lean back and simplify. Some seasons can be long and trying and others can be fleeting. The important thing is, remember that the season you're experiencing is serving a purpose for your future. Throughout the years I've noticed that for most of my clients, the hardest part isn't the sprint but the warm-up. They can deal and get through the overwhelming part, but when there is white space, they retreat back into their limited mindset. In a season of slowing, I remind clients this spaciousness is an opportunity to warm up for what's to come. Without a warm-up leading to the sprint, we're often prone to injury. This is also true in business. It's vital that we embrace seasons of rest rather than revert to fear and limited thinking and use the time to reflect, plan, and prepare for the sprint ahead.

Some seasons will be more conducive to fun, play, and rest, while others are more demanding. You may not have time to take a vacation with your girlfriends in the coming months, and this is okay! I know it's hard to feel you're missing out.

It takes confidence to get out of your way and acknowledge that in certain seasons (even with a time-abundance mindset) there just *won't* be enough time for everything. Your priorities will need to be adjusted. You will need to set boundaries with yourself and accept that you just can't do it all without burning out.

Are you in a season of increasing responsibilities? Ladies, sometimes all you can do is lean in. Maybe the ever-increasing to-do list is a result of using your time well—you've been warming up and believing for this for some time. As you juggle new roles, it's important that you come to terms with the fact that every season is temporary. Yes, you may be maxed out, but missing out on social gatherings, sleep, and hobbies is only temporary. The key to successfully handling full seasons is setting limits and releasing the guilt around doing so. In past seasons of sprinting, I spent hours beating myself up and regretting missed gatherings, feeling like such a bad friend, but today I can confidently say I know my limits. Choosing to accept my limitations in these kinds of seasons gave me the ability to persevere. Ladies, *you* can do this too!

Get Creative

Creativity is the key to everything. And it's an innate gift to every single person—all of us are capable of creatively solving problems. It's what arises when we need to think on our feet in a survival situation. It often requires that we ask for help, practice flexibility, and think outside of the box. Now if you're like me, asking others for help may not be your favorite thing to do. But in order to get past the lie that there isn't enough time, it's important to be creative with your time and flexible with your ego, which usually includes some form of asking for help or outsourcing. If you want more time, you've got to allow others to come alongside you and assist you in the hours that you do have. Many hands make light work, right?

Consider this quick exercise/mindset shift:

1. Make a list of all of the personal tasks you can outsource.
2. Ask yourself what your time is really worth. If you could free up time in one area, how much could you make in your business?
3. Figure out what tasks are the least expensive to pass off. For example, does your local grocery store offer grocery delivery for a small fee? With that grocery delivery service, you may say, "Yes, but I really don't want to pay the five dollars for delivery." I challenge you with this: Is an hour of your time not worth more than five dollars? Could you squeeze in another forty-five-minute client at one hundred dollars per hour rather than spending that time at the grocery store? That would most likely cover the delivery fee *and* pay for your groceries for the week! Ummm, win-win, ladies.

This also goes for laundry service and a housekeeper. During a busy season I found that dropping my laundry off cost just a few additional dollars each week but saved hours of my time.

I understand that you may feel that you're not in a season to invest in a meal prepping service or a housekeeper—I have been there. But when I calculated the amount of time the tasks would have taken me and how much it cost to outsource, I found that if I worked during those hours I would have spent "doing all the things," I could actually end up making more money. Maybe you are early in business and not yet bringing in an income. Even in this place I encourage you to consider the long-term benefit. Look for someone you can trade services with. Maybe there is a woman in your neighborhood who needs life coaching but can't afford it. She may be open to a housecleaning barter. Bottom line, get creative! When you are creative with time, you'll find a way to focus on what matters in your life and business.

The less time you have to work with, the more creative and boundaried you need to get with it. Today my time feels more abundant chasing two babies around than it ever did before I had kids. Yes, life is busy and very full—but I do have time for it all. When we learn to reframe our thinking, set boundaries, accept the time-barren seasons, and get creative with what we have, we are better at prioritizing our time and creating margin for what's most important. Ladies, let's walk away from this chapter telling ourselves, *We have MORE than enough time to accomplish our deepest longings and desires*!

LIE #10

It's Already Been Done Before

Several years ago I was asked to speak at a virtual Women in Business Summit. This event was a way for the organizer to market her mission, give back to her tribe, and introduce and connect women leaders with one another. The event took place pretty early on in my own business career when I hadn't yet developed the confidence that I have today. I remember looking at the lineup of speakers, including their qualifications, and feeling just a teensy bit like *they're already doing it—is there really space for me?*

Have you ever felt like the seat has already been taken by someone better than you? You set out to start something you felt was unique, only to find others are already doing it. You wonder:

- If I had just launched when I initially had the dream, I could have arrived there first. Am I too late now?

- Why can't anything I create feel original? I bet everyone sees me as a knockoff.
- What I talk about in my business has already been said before. What's so special about little old me?

Ladies, these are not valid reasons for playing small! When we get caught in a mindset of *This has already been done before—and probably better than I could do it*, we set ourselves up for failure from the get-go. We undermine our confidence in our business and ourselves, second-guess every decision, and set ourselves up for comparison and envy as we obsess over what others are doing. So let me help you debunk this limiting belief by offering four key ways to reframe your thinking and practical exercises to help broaden your business vision.

Nothing Is New

Nothing is original. Have you found yourself thinking about this as you prepare to launch or expand your business? Feeling deflated by the fact that we see similar ventures all around us, we may try to console ourselves with the thought that there's "nothing new under the sun," as they say. But in reality, this statement isn't entirely true. Yes, the thing you are doing or are about to embark on most likely already exists in some form—there are other entrepreneurs out there in your field providing similar services or products and catering to the same customers. However, *the way you are about to do it* is unique to you, and you alone.

Ever notice each week on the grocery line how all of the celebrity gossip magazines talk about the same darn things: "Inside Pictures of Her Mansion," "The Top Five Celebrity

Beach Bodies," "Real or Fake?," "She Finally Left Him," "Behind the Scenes, Never-Before-Seen Footage of Her Cellulite"?

I can't even type this with a straight face. You know exactly what I'm talking about! The magazines, the headlines, the candid shots are all essentially the same, yet people still purchase these magazines week after week. And why is this? Although the messages are pretty much the same, it's always someone different. While it may have been Reese Witherspoon this week, next week it may be Mandy Moore or Kerry Washington. It could be the same headline, but when it's someone different, we're compelled to pick up the magazine and read more! This may seem like a trivial example, but the underlying truth is powerful. Even if you're doing something that's already been done, it's different because there is no other you. Your business could be the mirror of hundreds of other businesses, but because the business is being run by you, it's unique. Maybe you've struggled with one of the following thoughts:

- I'm launching a health coaching program, but there are already thousands of other health coaches.
- There are already plenty of ice cream shops; what makes mine unique?
- The children's book that's been on my heart to write for years has already been published. Is there really room for mine?
- The internet is flooded with marketing agencies; what would make someone want to hire my team?

It can feel daunting when you see others doing the very thing you are passionate about. In the early days, it truly felt unique to you until you began looking elsewhere. Well, guess what? It still is. A dear friend and mentor, Amber Lilyestrom, always says, "If the dream is in you, it is for you." What if it is really that simple? If you can see the dream, you can create the dream, even if it's been done before. Ladies, there is plenty of room for YOU and here is why:

- No one, not anyone in this world, is YOU.
- No one has the same upbringing.
- No one has the exact same personality and temperament.
- No one has the same perspective.
- No one has walked the same path.
- Your story is different, unique to YOU, and this is what makes your purpose different from everyone else's.

Let's quickly circle back to those above examples. First, ice-cream shops have been around forever and continue to open. And each shop has its own twist on flavors (no pun intended!), ambiance, and way of doing things. Not even plain vanilla or chocolate is done exactly the same way. And the same goes for every business, even mine! There is an abundance of therapists and mindset coaches out there, but none are ME. Yes, it's the same business, but everything else is different, and this sets me apart.

I wholeheartedly believe there is more than enough room for your business to succeed, even if it's not the first of its kind! It's as simple as staying in your own lane, showing up authentically as yourself, and keeping your eye on the *impact* that you can create rather than the insecurities that come from comparing yourself to others. The entire package you encompass is what will attract or repel customers. This is why it is crucial to be unapologetic with your story, your beliefs, and your values. Marie Forleo says it best: "If you're tawkin' to everybody, you're tawkin' to nobody."[1] Ladies, when you allow your true colors to shine, you will naturally set yourself apart from the others!

Find Your Niche

Now that we've begun processing how to set ourselves apart, let's dig into the practical. How do you actually stand out from the others in your own special way? Find your niche. Niche? What the heck is that, and how does this apply to my business? Your niche is exactly what we've been discussing—your unique qualities that set you apart from the others. If you're not yet certain what your niche is, the key to discovering it is narrowing your focus. Try out these two exercises to see if you can hone in on what that means for you:

1. Think of something you could never grow tired of talking about. At first, you may think it is personal and unrelated to business, but I can assure you that it ties directly into your calling in business. For example, I've always loved to help and uplift people. I used to say it would be a dream to be able to help people solve problems and find peace in their lives while getting paid for it. I didn't think it could be possible, but I've tied it into the specific services that I offer, and so the work I do today is *exactly* that.

2. Take action. Often my clients will say, "Kate, how do I really, like really, know if this is my niche? I know it

excites me, but what if I'm wrong?" My answer: The only way to find out is to take consistent action. This can be done by beta testing if you have a service-based business. I always encourage my clients to create a focus group of participants to test out their service or products and collect honest feedback whenever they start a business or pivot their niche. By taking consistent, calculated steps to test out your niche, it will become apparent over time whether it feels right for you and your customers. And with time and practice, your confidence will grow. One word of advice—even after testing, be open to your niche shifting for you! It's possible to get bored or want to try something new. When I opened my therapy practice I knew my niche would be Dialectical Behavior Therapy because it was something I was trained in, confident in, and enjoyed doing. And with time, I decided to narrow my niche even more, offering DBT therapy just for adult clients. When I started I was working with adults and teens, but through *taking action* and practicing my niche, I realized that working with adults felt more effortless and aligned. Choosing a niche to set yourself apart makes your work feel effortless. And when your work feels effortless, it's a recipe for happy customers.

One common objection I get from clients is, "But if I choose a niche, I will be leaving people out." Ladies, this fear is common: that if you single people out and narrow your focus, there won't be enough customers for you. WRONG. I had a client who sold jewelry and accessories. In all of her marketing she spoke to women. However, around holidays such as

Valentine's Day, she found men were reaching out to place an order for a special female in their life. Just because you are marketing your message to a niche audience doesn't mean others won't become customers as well. I can't tell you how many men write to me and say they appreciate my podcast and the free content I offer, reminding me that not enough men are talking about this stuff. I even recently received a kind email from a gentleman who thanked me and asked if I had any recommendations of men who do similar work. So, ladies, it doesn't mean you won't attract a variety of clients just because you are choosing a niche and speaking to a very specific audience.

Gain Confidence to Move Out in a Crowded Field

Like they say, the grass isn't greener on the other side, it's greenest where we water it. Are you too busy looking at what everyone else is doing rather than stewarding what you already have? In the early stages of my coaching business I remember being guarded, alert to who was doing something similar and who might be copying me. I spent hours feeling stuck and disappointed when I thought someone was trying to knock off my work. Little did I know that I was guilty of this myself—using others' work as inspiration for my own.

It wasn't until I was going through the book *31 Days of Prayer for the Dreamer and the Doer*, by Jenn (Sprinkle) Jett and Kelly Rucker,[2] and read a passage about low confidence and comparison that I was able to shift my thinking. Remember the whole nothing-is-original speech? What you have created has already been done before, just not by you. In time, I realized that it wasn't about copying; it's only natural to admire someone else's ideas and be inspired. If something similar is already in full bloom, use this as validation that the concept *is* working and there still is room for your spin on it. This new viewpoint gave me permission to love the women around me who were offering similar products and services, because I now believed there were plenty of seats at the table.

Feeling like there isn't enough room at the table or worrying about others copying your work is actually a manifestation of low confidence. It's rooted in a fearful belief that we aren't good enough and that our product or business won't stand on its own merits. If you've struggled with these thoughts before, here are two quick ways to overcome these limited mindsets:

1. Begin cheering for the success of others. I know, when you are deeply invested in your work, this doesn't always feel possible or exciting. *I only want to champion my own success, because if I cheer for her and she succeeds, it's taking away from me*, you may think. WRONG. Remember the idea of an abundance mindset? There is *enough* room for both of you—there is always more than enough success to go around. In order to grow your confidence, you must continually tell yourself there's plenty of room for you. Back when I was so fixated on others copying me, I vowed that anytime I caught myself in this mindset, I would replace my own insecurities with a prayer for that woman's success. Maybe for you, it's sending an encouraging note or taking a moment to wish someone well. Let me tell you, it's a game changer. It will solidify an abundance mindset, softening your heart to allow deep friendships and community to flow in and flourish.

2. Quit being selfish. Okay, this one may hit a few
   nerves—but let me explain. Holding on to your gift
   out of fear that there's no room for it, or for any other
   reason, is preventing someone who needs it from receiving it. When I feel afraid about a new endeavor,
   I stop myself and say, *Kate, quit being so selfish. This is
   your gift to share. It's not about you. Think of the lives
   that can be changed if you step out and offer it to the
   world.* This mantra gives me the biggest kick in the
   rear to get out of my own way and move forward, even
   if the confidence isn't fully there. As we touched on
   earlier in the book: do the thing and then the bravery
   will follow. If you believe in your mission, who are you
   to withhold that good gift from the world?

I always tell my clients that like most things in life, confidence is not something you are born with. It's a muscle that
needs to constantly be worked. With time, patience, consistency, and application, it will begin to develop, *and* never
stop developing. Each and every time you approach a new
confidence challenge, take it as a sign of growth. If you are
uncomfortable, it means you aren't standing still. And if you're
not standing still, you're moving and on a path to accomplish
what you set out to accomplish.

Embrace Collaboration Rather than Competition

Friendships are important not only in life, but also in business. I believe it's vital that we link arms with others who are
striving for something similar. I know this sounds terrifying
for some of you. *Why would I link arms with someone who may*

want the same thing as me and could potentially be my competition? Again, because there is more than enough space for each of us to succeed in this world. And when we join together in collaboration, we actually enhance each other's unique gifts.

Something I want to encourage you to do is find your tribe. Who are those women you can go to for accountability, encouragement, celebrations, etc.? Many of the women I work with voice feeling incapable of finding their supporters. I encourage them to look for small communities where this type of connection is encouraged. Nowadays there are tons of free support groups locally and on the internet for business-minded women. If you can't find one, you can find another person and start one! These kinds of relationships have been the lifeline of my business. Entrepreneurship can feel especially lonely if you are used to going to an office full of people for your job. I have built some of these relationships by simply asking someone if I could sit at her table at a coffee shop with my laptop, and you can too!

The more we connect with other women, cheer them on, and offer to help support their mission, the greater the reach we have together. When people ask what my secret is to growing my business and tribe, I tell them it's collaboration over competition. You can let go of hoarding and open your hands to freely give without fear of someone doing it better. And ladies, it's so simple! For example, you and a colleague may both have different audiences of two thousand people each. You can host a joint project and rather than reaching just two thousand, you now have an audience of four thousand.

Each of us has unique gifts and talents. Each of us has a different story. Each of us has a different temperament—Myers Briggs, Love Language, Enneagram, etc. The bottom line? We are *all* different. Some of us are good in certain areas and not so good in others. Collaboration is linking arms and saying, "I know you excel in this area and could use some help in another. I'm really good in that area and find it fun and fulfilling to fill those gaps for you." Collaboration does just that—it fills the gaps.

We all have gaps—although we may not like to admit it. It's often easier to ignore the places where we struggle and forge ahead, focusing instead on our strong suits. But if you can identify areas of weakness and allow others to support you, you'll have a much stronger and more well-rounded business. And because you can offer support in their areas of weakness, you both benefit. Let's pause for a quick exercise to help you identify possible gaps.

Write down the top five things you really pride yourself on. Maybe it's business systems, event planning, cooking meals, or even offering the gift of encouragement. For me, it feels so effortless to send a quick voice message with pointers and insights to a friend when they're struggling with limited thinking. What are your top five?

1. _____
2. _____
3. _____
4. _____
5. _____

Now take a moment and think of those gaps—places where the struggle is real. What are those things that you dread doing? You know—the ones that take up way too much of your brain space and time. These may be the very things that others in your circle can easily do with their eyes closed. For example, my forte is neither tech nor systems, so I will accept help in these areas whenever offered! What are the top five areas around which you could accept support?

1. _____
2. _____
3. _____
4. _____
5. _____

Now I want to challenge you to snap a photo of this page and text it to your inner circle of business friends. Who are those ladies who are your champions, your dream defenders, your accountability sisters? I'm sure you all have multiple things on those lists that can be swapped—you help someone in one of your five power areas, and she helps you in one of your gaps—to create deeper and even more gratifying relationships.

Putting It All Together

Remember my opening story about questioning my ability to add something valuable, asking myself why there would be room for me to speak at the Women in Business Summit? Well, rather than get all caught up in comparison and doubt, I decided to wish the best for all of the women speaking, acknowledge that there was space for me, and, despite still having doubts, speak at the summit anyway. This is key: even when the feeling of inadequacy hits, *do it anyway*. We can choose whether we give in to fear or take bold action—and by shifting your mindset around the lie of scarcity or inadequacy, you'll be empowered to take that action every time.

And you'll be amazed at what taking action can reap. Over a year after the summit, one of the speakers sent me a message out of the blue. I was thrilled—this speaker was not only the author of a bestselling book but also someone I admired for her incredible influence and heart for encouraging women, how she navigated motherhood gracefully, and how she captivated audiences through her speaking. Her message went something like this:

> Kate, I know this might sound odd, but your name came to mind the other day and I felt a nudge to reach out to you. I saw you are in the trenches of proposal writing for your book, and I've been there before. I've recently been working to accelerate my business and feel I could use some slight steering. I know this might sound crazy, please go think about it and pray about it, but I feel something telling me that we are supposed to join hands and help each other.

You know those moments when something grabs your attention to show you that what's in front of you is for you? Well, that was this moment. I began to cry and knew instantly I would respond with an enthusiastic *yes*. Earlier that month I had just received my first few rejections in the agent pitching process and was feeling disheartened. I needed confirmation to keep going. Well, this sign was delivered right when I needed it most, after those rejections, when the doubt hit the hardest.

Because the summit speaker (my friend) took action (scary as it might have been for her), we were able to link arms and fill in those gaps for one another. If she hadn't taken that bold risk of possible rejection, there's a chance that this book you're holding in your hands wouldn't be here today and that her trajectory in her business could have looked a lot different. Just to show you the impact of our linking arms to help one another—her business has grown exponentially and her husband was able to quit his job in order to homeschool the kids. How incredible is this?

She and I talk all the time about how *easy* it felt to support one another. Her helping me refine my pitches to agencies and my helping her get her coaching programs off the ground felt fun and life-giving to us both. We all have specific skills that we can share with others. And ladies, this is just one story of how my accountability sisters and fellow bosses have filled in the gaps for me. I can honestly say that this business would not be where it is today if it weren't for the support and collaborative spirit of my tribe. But I wouldn't have found them if I had viewed other business owners as competition. They have pitched in, filling in the gaps for me. And they've shared that I've done the same for them. My gift of helping others see things differently through perspective shifts comes naturally and easily to me, so why would I hold on to it when I can help others?

Are you blocking yourself from potential friendships and support systems because you're afraid others may steal your idea or spotlight? Let go of that fear today, and open your hands to receive the gifts of others.

Final Thoughts

When it comes to owning who you are and having confidence in your business, it all starts with *showing up*. In order to attract the right people, you need to show up exactly as you are each day. If dressing up, wearing high heels, putting on lipstick, and giving your hair a fresh blowout is what feels true to you, then this is how you must show up. If kicking off your first meeting of the day in yoga pants, flip-flops, and a dry-shampooed topknot, with a green juice in hand, feels true to you, then you do you! The secret to success is accepting there is no right or wrong way to show up and do things in your business—the key is simply showing up authentically. *That's* what sets you apart. There are a ton of mindset coaches out there; however, not all show up to their Facebook lives with a three-ring circus in the background. Not all share their story of healing and recovery. Not all are petrified to speak to large crowds of people. And not all show up in the everyday chaos of life unapologetically.

In closing, I want to encourage you to take some time to sit and journal about what makes you unique. Here are some prompts to get you thinking:

- What is unique about my upbringing?
- What is unique about my appearance and the way I present myself?
- What is unique about how I overcame my biggest struggle?
- What is unique about the training, expertise, or schooling I have?
- How am I unique as a friend, family member, significant other, etc.?
- What do others tell me is unique about me?
- How is my business different from others?

- How is my client or customer experience different from others?

Do you know anyone else who can answer these questions exactly like you? I doubt it. Your answers are different from mine. Now take all of the above questions and combine them in a short paragraph below. When you are done, complete your paragraph with this sentence: *I am forever grateful for being wonderfully unique. I have the gift of showing up in this world exactly as I am.*

_____

_____

_____

_____

_____

_____

_____

How did it feel doing this exercise? Can you see how you add a unique twist to all that you do? We can all shine our lights without outshining someone else's. There is more than enough space for your business, your mission, your impact that you are set out and called to create in this world. Quit dimming your light and shying away because you think someone else is already doing it. Remember, you *are* original. What you are creating has never been or ever will be done exactly as you are doing it. So create a scene. Make your mark. Show up exactly as you are each and every day and not only will you stand apart, but you will feel the most *you*. By leaning into your truest self, you'll have more confidence in your work, offer a better product, and be more willing to join with your fellow bosses to move forward. When we choose collaboration over competition, we light a spark for even more to come. So that boss lady you've been wanting to reach out to but you've been hesitating? Run toward her, stand next to her, link arms with her, and find a way to use your unique twist to enhance her mission and yours! You've got this.

LIE #11

I Am My Business

J
ust one more email and I'll be done for the night, babe," I yell down the hall to my husband. Except one email turns into two, which leads me to remember I have one last comment to address in my Confident Ladies Club community. As I'm commenting, I realize that the topic is solid content for an Instagram post, and ya gotta repurpose as much as possible, am I right ladies? I quickly create an Instagram post, then I notice my direct message box indicates new messages. I respond to a few simple questions, but then I see an inquiry for my services and feel the urge to respond right back. I mean, I don't want to miss out on a new customer. I then realize I need to update my online scheduling system for the week to make space for conversations with potential new clients. Before I know it, two more hours have passed. It's now 9:45 p.m., and I still haven't showered for the day.

I walk into the family room and announce I am done with work for the night. My husband sighs, and then begins a familiar lecture: "When are you going to start detaching from your business, Kate? You literally work around the clock. You left your full-time job so that you could have more flexibility, and this looks like the complete opposite."

It isn't worth arguing; I had already accepted that this was my new normal. In order to be successful in life, and specifically this business, I was told I needed to make sacrifices. *In time*, I tell myself, *I'm sure he'll begin to understand, and this will just become our new normal as a family. I chose this path and have accepted that I am now my business.*

Can anyone else relate? You no longer feel a distinction between your work and your life—it all feels like one continual day, and your identity is your business. The things you used to love, the hobbies you once had, the outings you enjoyed, and the vacations you used to organize—they are no longer significant. Though you can't see it, the business *passion* has now turned into *obsession*. It's all that you know, and it's the only thing capable of providing comfort in your life. The parts of your nonwork life that you used to love are now obligations. They feel like roadblocks disrupting the path you have decided to go down. This is the place where many entrepreneurs begin withdrawing from life and welcoming in the mindset of *I am my business and my identity lies within it.*

The sneaky thing about this mindset is that it will whisper to you that nothing else matters. As an entrepreneur, you feel a constant pull to your work. You could always be doing more, even when you're feeling completely maxed out mentally. You lie in bed at night, your brain still spinning with ideas, tasks you left unfinished, strategies you need to implement. Maybe you notice it in your relationships—you and your husband are constantly bickering, or maybe your friendships have been relegated to the back burner. Perhaps it shows up in your health—because you're so immersed in your business, little by little your health habits are falling to the wayside. You find yourself working through lunch, skimping on sleep to meet deadlines, not exercising because you're overbooked with meetings, or not leaving the house for days at a time because this one last thing has to get wrapped up.

Often we're numb to it all. You don't actually notice these new habits until someone else points them out to you. At first you feel defensive, but then a week or two later you begin to wonder if it may be true. You find yourself trying to justify your consuming work habits. *I love my business so much. It's worth cutting corners in other areas of my life. I can focus on those down the road, but this is what I need to be successful for now.* You love your business immensely, and it never quite feels like work—the very reason you can't turn off. It feeds your soul, and yet . . . it never stops. You identify this current season as one of ambitious hustle—which we all know is a load of you know what. This one isn't just a season, it has become your lifestyle. You always believed that in order to be successful, you must work for it. Somewhere along the way, you may have taken this belief a little too far.

Taking Your Pulse

Before we dive into debunking this mindset, let's get the lay of the land when it comes to your relationship with your business. Consider the following questions:

- Are you proud of the relationship you have with your business, or would you rather have more balance between work and personal life?

- Who were you before you had your business? Do you still have an identity outside of your business?

If you are unable to clearly answer these questions, please don't panic. Most lady bosses I work with need some time to reflect and respond. For one, many don't know their own work boundaries, and two, many are either ashamed of their work-life balance or even in denial that it's unhealthy.

I know today it may feel impossible to imagine having some sort of balance in your business, but I want to tell you that it is possible. The truth is, you didn't go from employee to entrepreneur to work twice as much. I'm also sure you knew that the flexible and effortless entrepreneurial life depicted on social media (that we see so often) doesn't happen overnight or possibly ever. Ladies, don't believe all that you see! What is possible for most is something in the middle—owning a profitable business and having a life without sacrificing your sanity. And in order to get there, it takes trial and error. It takes falling down and getting back up. It takes great flexibility and extending loads of grace to yourself. It takes getting to a place where you can actually have a love for both business and life.

So how can we create a distinction between loving our business and loving our life? It's a big question—and one that will be constantly shifting from one season to the next. As we've talked about, there will be seasons of hustle and seasons of rest. And these transitional seasons will have a direct effect on your perspective. No one has mastered the art of balance. Let me repeat that: *no* one has mastered it, so quit beating yourself up for not finding it yet. Life is about give-and-take and resting in the fluidity it contains. That said, there are guidelines we can implement to help us distinguish between our business and ourselves—and flourish fully in both.

I have two areas I want to tackle with you: first, getting clear on your identity outside of your business, and second, gaining clarity around your business balance. As we work through each of these, my hope is that you'll be able to get a clear understanding of what you want your business life "balance" to look like in this season and develop flexibility for the seasons ahead.

Your Identity Is Not Tied to Your Business Success

Back in 2015, on a weekly accountability call with my business bestie, I caught myself saying something pretty disturbing. I'm quite honestly feeling the feelings again even repeating what I said, but this book's about vulnerability, so here we go. "I've gotta hustle, I've gotta get to that next level, because I would rather die than go back to a nine-to-five. I would be such a failure if that had to happen. There's no way I'd want to face the people around me."

I wish that I could say I was joking, but I really felt trapped. I felt that if this business failed, it would mean that I failed at life. And if I failed at life, I'd have no reason to live. My entire identity lay within my business. If you ever hear a business friend or anyone in your life talking this way about their business or career, please pay close attention and encourage them to get help. And you may be in this space today. If so, I want you to know that I understand. It doesn't have to be this way. Your identity does not lie in how much work or money you can produce. When I think back to that day and that entire season, I realize I was living in immense fear.

This was the motto I was living by: *If I don't work around the clock, I will lose my business. If I lose my business, I am no longer a somebody in this world, and therefore I will have no value.*

When we think about taking a step back to find more balance, we often experience this kind of thinking. If I'm not giving *everything* to my business, will I be *anything?* It's a dangerous mindset. So how can we balance our business with the rest of our life, while still holding on to our identity? Let's begin by circling back to two questions from earlier in the chapter: Who were you before you had your business? Do you still have an identity outside of your business today?

How would you answer these questions? In the six months that I typically work with my clients, each and every one of them hits a place where they realize that they don't have any idea of what lights them up outside of their work. They report that they no longer find joy in the hobbies and activities they once loved. When I suggest that they take some time to unplug from business to do something fun, they are often unable to tell me what fun looks like for them.

Not too long ago I was in this space myself—as that phone call with my friend illustrates. My sense of meaning, purpose, and enjoyment all lay within the business. When things went right in business, I was happy. When I made money, I was happy. When I was offered business opportunities, I was happy. I no longer needed hobbies or people to bring me joy. Finding my happiness within my business seemed so easy— like a one-stop shop. I no longer needed to put forth effort and engage in things outside of work to bring me joy, I could find it all in this one place. It seemed perfect! But this kind of thinking is dangerous because it shifts our attention inward. It pulls us from the greater tapestry of our life—our family, friends, neighborhood, wider community—and shrinks our focus to business and business only.

Here's the truth: Your business success does not define your identity. If your business idea fails, you are not a failure. And this is why it is so important that we do not neglect our life outside of our business. Whether we succeed or fail in business does not determine whether we are a success or a failure as a person. This is why it is crucial that we cultivate balance so that when an idea does fail (I say *when* because it's bound to happen!), we can get right back up, confident that our worthiness is unchanged.

Your Ideal Business

By now you may be in that place where you can acknowledge that your business is running you. You feel tired, burned out, and completely lifeless. The adrenaline is waning and you're crashing hard. You may feel tense, bracing for others to say, "I told you so." Take heart: you're not alone. Many entrepreneurs fall into the burnout trap. If you own a business, you are passionate about something. Passionate people easily get swept away in the excitement and possibility of the dream coming to fruition. Think of falling in love and letting your guard down maybe a little too soon. This is what so many of us do in our business. We see the potential, get caught up in the excitement, and want to run with it and give it our all. And when this occurs, it's easy to lose our intentionality, slipping into something that is less than ideal.

Let's look at that first crucial question again: Are you proud of the relationship you have with your business, or would you rather have more balance between work and personal life?

So many women have trouble answering this question. But at its root, it simply boils down to what I have been asking you throughout this book: What do YOU really want? Take a moment and personalize the following for yourself:

What do I, _____ [insert your name], *really want in my ideal business?*

_____

_____

_____

State it and claim it!

Ladies, this question should be a weekly reminder, if not a daily question you ask yourself. It's so easy to become immersed in all the things in your business and fail to check in to see if what you are doing is still aligned and truly what you want. When we are going through the motions, we tend to miss the bigger picture. And when this happens, our confidence decreases and we begin to question whether we are deserving of what it is we desire. I've seen it time and time again with my clients. They tell themselves they are flawed in some way. In this state of vulnerability they begin to think that everyone else deserves to get what they want in business *except* them. Do you believe that you actually can get what you want, or have you assumed that only special people get what they want? I am here to assure you today that the way you run your business and what you reap from it is a choice.

It may be challenging to define your ideal business, but now that we've highlighted what *isn't aligned* for you, maybe you can relate to one of these:

- You are on the brink of quitting your business of six years because you feel completely helpless, too far gone, and that you will never get a grasp on shaping it into something that is ideal for you and your dream lifestyle.
- You have lost sight of your WHY. You began the business with a mission in mind, and now you're merely surviving. You scrape by each day to pay the bills, meet deadlines, and keep up with all of the administrative tasks within your business.

The sky is the limit when running a business. If we aren't happy with the way things are, we can make changes. We have the freedom to decide what our business commitment looks like based on our season in life, our income goals, and how quickly we want to make things happen. In order to find out just how we want our business to look and what it will take to get there, let's dig into these questions:

- How much time are you putting into your business?
- How much money are you making?
- How long have you been running your business?
- Do you have staff and systems in place? If yes, what does this look like?
- What does your personal life look like?
- What is your work schedule? Do you have set days and hours that you work? How about vacation, sick time, and family leave time?

After answering these, consider the following: Is this what you really want? Do you feel fulfilled running your business this way? If money weren't an issue for you, would you still be working this way?

Chances are, the answer may be "no." Some of you may even be in tears after writing this out because you've been so absorbed in your success that you haven't given yourself time to step away and get a bird's-eye view of your life. You've been doing everything you can to keep your head above water.

Don't panic! With some intentionality, you can steer the ship of your business and life into a space that feels more manageable, life-giving, and balanced. And it starts with giving voice to just what that means for you. If you lived in an ideal world and could run your business in a way that feels more fulfilling, what would that look like? Take some time to write out what that dream business would look like:

_____

_____

_____

_____

_____

_____

Hold on to this vision, ladies, and remind yourself of the life you really want. It *is* attainable—you just have to kick out some junk first.

Now Let's Apply This Like a Boss

As we continue to uproot this lie, let's take a step back and look at the big picture. Let's go back to the ideal business visualization. Grab it and hold on to it while you go through these next steps to move yourself toward that healthier, more balanced life. So where do you start?

Set Limits around Your Work Hours

Do you want a set work schedule, or do you want business to organically blend with life? There is no right answer here. You've got to choose what feels right for you in this season. In my first business, I wanted to create a distinction between work and personal hours, yet in my current business, I love having a flexible work schedule. In order to run my current business efficiently, I have needed to set boundaries with myself and not take on clients every day of the week. I know a day will come when I may want a more structured schedule again, but right now this is what works for our family. I've gone from working all day every day (yes, including weekends) to working in little pockets of time. Kids are now my full-time gig, and my business flows around that. There are days where I have zero childcare, and there are days when I have help. Through this transitional season I've learned to utilize whatever windows of time I can get. At times this is setting an alarm to wake up at 3 a.m. to finish a chapter or doing work in a parking lot with a sleeping baby in the car. Because I am embracing a flexible schedule in this more time-barren season, I don't quite feel like I'm ever fully "off" work, but again, this is how I am making things work in this busy season—I know that it won't be forever!

Ask Yourself, Am I Being Realistic?

I find many entrepreneurs place super-high expectations on themselves that aren't congruent with their lifestyle. You may be in a season with less time than you have been used to. Maybe you are caring for a sick parent and that sixty hours per week you had to devote to your business has been knocked down to twenty. You find yourself frustrated because the goals you set earlier in the year aren't being hit, yet you are forgetting you are working with a third of the time. This happened to me with my first baby. The time I had to devote to business went from seventy hours to ten to twelve hours per week, yet my expectations for myself were the same. I was continually frustrated. This makes no sense at all, and it's where I needed to adjust. Start by asking yourself, *Am I being realistic? Are my goals at the moment congruent with my lifestyle?* And if not, you can give yourself grace, adjust your expectations, and make the necessary changes.

Set Limits with Others and Self

After having my first baby, I implemented the first two steps and then realized that in order to realistically run my business in the fashion I wanted, I needed to begin setting greater boundaries. Are you sensing a theme in this book? Boundaries are essential—whether it's to safeguard your time, protect your relationships, or build the work-life balance you want, you've got to embrace the lifelong skill of boundary setting. When it came to disentangling my identity from my business, I realized I had to take some time to evaluate my commitments and activities so that I had some margin outside of my business. Were all of my commitments necessary? Did I have to give so much of myself to my business, or could I redirect some of that energy elsewhere? I sat down, did the math, and evaluated the behaviors and routines that were happening merely out of habit, by default. It became clear that in order to balance my life and my business, I needed to simplify. I began doing only what was essential in my business so that I had time to devote to my identity and life outside of work.

Through this process, I also found greater clarity in my business, realizing there were tasks and events that were essential to increasing profits. The number one income-producing activity was relationship building. This was done by showing up on my social media channels and interacting with others. And so I began focusing my energy on this. Ladies, I got clear. I simplified. I put my foot down and said no more doing all the things I think I have to do in order to be successful. I told myself that just because it worked for someone else doesn't mean it worked for me. I began believing that I could create success *and* have a life. And because I set these boundaries with myself, I created more success in my business *and* in my life.

Going Deeper

Now that you have the tools to work on the outer, more tangible steps, let's go a little deeper and explore ways to reconnect with ourselves outside of our business.

Remember What Used to Light You Up

Think back to the inner child visualization from the introduction of this book. If you recall, we went way back to your first life memories to recall what brought you life at a young age. Typically, those things that were life-giving to you as a child will be life-giving to you in some way as an adult. As you reconnect with your identity and what you really want in life, returning to these activities can help you access what once brought you joy.

Maybe you used to get really excited about creating art projects with your babysitter. You would sit for hours with your little paintbrush and paint-by-numbers book. Today, I suggest you look for one of those fun painting and wine classes. If such a thought makes you cringe—maybe you're in a place in life where you feel like you no longer have friends because you've been so immersed in your business; or maybe such an activity feels childish or like you're wasting time—that's okay. This is an opportunity for you to get out of your comfort zone, meet some people, and reconnect with things that bring you joy. You also never know who you may bump into at a place like this. You may fully intend to not talk about work, but you could end up meeting a new business connection. Or maybe you'll find more relaxation and simple joy than you've had in months. As you allow yourself to just live and enjoy life, you'll find blessings you never expected.

Or maybe it's something else. Did you love to dance as a child? You could sign up for a dance class. Maybe your childhood self loved playing Pretty Pretty Princess; reach out to that business connection who sells Stella and Dot jewelry and request to host a trunk party for a few girlfriends or even your business besties! Maybe you loved to sing and play piano; now that could look like hosting a karaoke night or getting back on the piano.

I can already hear you protesting: "I have so much on my plate! Why would I add one more thing—especially something frivolous?" Although the thought of committing to any of these may feel like work today, I can assure you that once you are in that moment, away from the screen, you will begin to see the importance of allowing activities like these back into your life. You may even experience a little sadness because of the realization that you've been missing out for a while, but it's never too late. Celebrate that you are starting fresh today. When I walk clients through this process, there is often an audible shift in their tone of voice as they have this realization. It's like a weight has been lifted and they can breathe again. They let go of guilt and awaken to the new mindset that fun is not frivolous but *good* for their life and their business. And with time, they get better at creating more space and margin for the things that bring joy.

What Currently Lights You Up?

What are some aspects of your business that bring you joy, and what in life do you want to find time for? For me, it's community—getting to spend time interacting with other heart-centered businesswomen. However, my work can sometimes feel isolating because it is all online. A couple of years ago I committed to hosting in-person lady boss events to get me away from the screen for one day per quarter and build community with other women. I didn't want these occasions to feel like your average networking event. I told the women: no nametags, no elevator pitches, no theme of discussion, just a gathering of women in business getting together to eat, unplug from the screen, and casually talk about big hopes and dreams. Women began traveling from hours away to attend these special gatherings in my home! These events bring me so much life. We connect about business—but also so much more, from home decorating to puppies to the latest beauty trends . . . you get the picture!

Going back to what brought you joy in the past and what fills your cup today is a great way to expand your fulfillment beyond your business. Because even when we know these are beneficial things for us to engage in, we often hold back in fear that we're wasting our time or being frivolous. We let guilt tell us that we don't deserve the time off. It feels counterproductive to take time to have fun when the never-ending to-do list still exists. We may even know it could be beneficial for our business, but we still find it hard to do. Day after day we stay glued to the screen, believing that we are doing what's best for our business, rather than giving ourselves permission to do business from a different angle.

"How is unplugging from my business still doing business?" I hear this question often. I refer to each of the examples I shared above as "business-building activities." Typically in business we think of the business-building activities as things like updating our websites, completing reports, meeting with vendors, etc. We don't think that doing life could possibly fall within this bracket, but I'm here to tell you that in fact it does. And often these not-so-typical business-building activities can be the best ones for your business. Here's why:

- In order to think clearly, we need to walk away from the work from time to time. There is wonder in the magic of letting go and stepping away.
- When you are truly happy and fulfilled by outside things, your energy is magnetic and will effortlessly trickle into your business.
- The best business ideas are almost always created outside of the business. (This one is 100 percent true for me.)

- Staying in hibernation can only take you so far. There is something so powerful about being with others in community. I get the warm fuzzies every time I spend time with my businesspeople and loved ones in person.

How would it feel if you could begin living your life for *you*, free from needing to be *in* your business 24/7 to feel productive or valuable? How would it feel to find your identity away from the office?

It may be daunting, but start by taking baby steps. It can happen little by little. As you implement small changes, you will find yourself in a space of greater balance and freedom. Today I love doing things outside of my business. I am confident that I wasn't created to live my life in isolation but rather to be in community with others. Looking back, I want to wrap a big warm blanket around that earlier version of myself. And for those of you struggling today, I am offering my blanket of compassion to you. If you feel enslaved by your business or constantly needing to prove yourself with certain business outcomes, I want you to know that it doesn't have to be this way. You are capable of building a fulfilling business *and* life that you love with your identity rooted in who you are, not what you produce—you don't have to live in fear!

LIE #12

I Am Not Capable
of Handling Success

For far too long I believed every one of the lies in this book, which all encompassed the greatest lie of all: *I am not capable of handling success.* On April 27, 2016, it became evident that I could check this one off my list as well. Everything I had ever dreamed of for my business was finally at my fingertips. Now ladies, let's get real; I hadn't built a Fortune 500 company or invented a medical cure, but for me, I really felt like I had made it. When I had envisioned this moment, I always imagined sharing a big, celebratory win with the people closest to me through a text message, over the phone, or maybe even with a glass of bubbly in person. But as I stared at my phone considering who I would text to celebrate with, I came to the stark realization that I had no one but me. I used to say I would never be one of those people who achieved all the success in the world and had no one to share it with. But in this moment, it was evident I had slipped into a scenario that I had hoped would never be true.

Succumbing to Fear

I've always been fascinated with the trajectory of success stories, comparing the one-hit wonders to the continual thrivers. In my years of one-on-one work with entrepreneurs, I've found that there are two types of people out there:

1. Those who say they want success but sabotage themselves because deep down they are fearful of what success may feel like. Many people fall into this category because it's easier to stay where it's familiar than to enter into the unknown. These people may look successful from the outside, but deep down they know their potential is far greater than their current performance.
2. Those who are also fearful of success, yet they recognize when self-sabotaging behavior begins to surface (because it is only natural for us to want to avoid discomfort), and they choose to continue moving toward their dreams and goals in spite of fear. These individuals know that they must do the work to face their fears, moving *through* discomfort and the unknown that can come with success.

Before we talk more about how we sabotage ourselves, pause to meditate on these simple questions: *What if I succeed at that big lofty goal I've been working toward? What am I willing to give up in order to have what I say I want? How will my life change, and how will that impact who I am and how I live?* And after doing so, ask yourself this: *Am I succumbing to fear and sabotaging my success? Why?* Take some time to reflect below:

I applaud you for getting vulnerable and answering these questions. Why do so many women fall into the deep, dark pit of fear around the thing they ultimately want in life? The simple answer is that they can't comprehend what life could be like for them on the other side. Here are some of the most common reasons I've heard throughout the years:

- If I succeed, I will lose all my friends.
- If I succeed, I won't be able to keep up.
- If I succeed, I may out-earn my partner.
- If I succeed, I will no longer be humble.

Do you see where this is going? It simply boils down to this: although where you're at today may not feel ideal, it's safe. I know it's hard. I've struggled with every one of the twelve lies I've shared with you. But success doesn't happen by accident—it takes intentionality and *doing the work* to reach our full potential. We *choose* to continually move forward, refusing to let lies and fear hinder our next steps. If I can do it, I know that you can too.

If I Succeed, I Will Lose All of My Friends

Now let's back up to that opening story of me scrolling through my phone, throwing a pity party because I had no one to share my success with. Remember it? Well, I'm going to share a secret with you. That story wasn't real. Okay, let's step back. The story was real, but not quite to the extreme of how it was told. It was told through the lens of how I viewed my circumstances, because at the time I didn't *believe* that I could experience success and still have the vibrant, supportive community and friendships that I cherished. So as I stared at my phone wondering whom I would text in that moment of pure panic, it *was* the reality I was living in my mind—I believed I had lost all of my friends and had no one to share my special moment with.

I'm grateful that this was not the truth but rather a slippery slope of my mindset during that season of my life. I was afraid of success because I believed that if I had a thriving business, I wouldn't be able to handle my friendships, and in turn, would lose them. I could have allowed my mind to continue running with this story, but in all circumstances, we have a choice. And I decided that this wasn't going to be my story. Moving forward

I adopted the mindset that friends are there to celebrate successes, and I will no longer hold back in fear of judgment.

If I Succeed, I Won't Be Able to Keep Up

"Wow. I can't believe this is why I've been holding back, but it makes complete sense now. All along I've been afraid of succeeding because I'm afraid of how uncomfortable it will feel to have what it is that I want. I don't know if I'll be able to keep up."

Can you relate? This is a pretty common conversation among the women I work with. When you're inching closer to the finish line, it can feel scary to envision what that new life may look like and how you will keep up. It's so easy for us to put our success on the back burner because we can't quite envision what living a new lifestyle will entail and if we will even have the mental capacity to handle it. Yet here's the thing: it is not possible to fathom what it will be like until we're actually *there,* living out those new goals in a new season.

Years ago I read a book called *The Big Leap,* by Gay Hendricks.[1] In this book he specifically talks about something he calls "upper limiting"—the imaginary glass ceiling we create to keep us safe from what we see as the burdens that come with success. We are programmed to believe that increased success equals a more complicated life, and so it's more comfortable to avoid it. However, it's important to remember that the success you've reached today is because of the beliefs and actions from a former version of you. For example, let's say two years ago you told yourself, *I want to take my online clothing boutique to a brick-and-mortar location,* and today you have done so. Back then, it felt like a lofty goal that would take time to

199

reach, and today it has become your new normal. Now you've been operating this brick-and-mortar business successfully for some time and want to open more locations, but it feels terrifying. Not reaching further out of an inability to envision a new normal is upper limiting. Can you see how not dreaming bigger is essentially keeping you stuck in past thinking? If you're experiencing this, just know that most people do! If you are not challenging yourself daily, you are living in the former version of you.

Personally, I experience this when I've accomplished a stretch goal. For the longest time the goal felt out of reach because it was a future version of me I was working toward. As I reach accomplishments, I easily forget to begin acting at a higher level of thinking—I am no longer in the past. And in order to do this, I need to begin visualizing the next new version of me to begin working toward. If you're struggling with this, it's important that you work through the exercises in the "Fake It Till You Become It" section of Lie #1 to help you get comfortable and believe for an even more robust version of yourself.

Going back to the clothing boutique scenario, having multiple locations will require you to majorly up-level your vision. How will you be spending your time if you have multiple locations? What will you need to cut out of your life to prioritize and welcome more space to operate at this level? What additional leadership qualities may you need to develop in order to oversee multiple locations of employees? Take the time to visualize how you will need to change the way you operate your thinking today in order to fully show up as that more robust version of yourself, who is capable of handling these new challenges.

I will say that when you are envisioning future success, it can be difficult to imagine what life will be like. Before being a business owner, I couldn't imagine how I would handle the responsibility of a business. I couldn't visualize what it would look like. It felt scary to imagine whether I could keep up with the responsibilities and earn enough income to pay the bills. Yet today, it doesn't faze me one bit. Going through the challenges and flexing my mindset muscles are what enabled me to believe in my own capabilities to handle new situations. After continually falling and getting back up, I now have the confidence that when challenges arise I will figure it out and be capable of keeping up. Fearing you won't be able to keep up if you find success can be easily disarmed by looking at past experiences and using them as future evidence that you in fact CAN keep up. Maybe not as gracefully as you hope, but you can and will keep up.

Take a moment to think back to a time when you were on the brink of a new level of success. What were your fears? How did it play out for you? How does your life look today, and how have you been able to manage? Take a few minutes to jot down your thoughts and realizations below:

If I Succeed, I May Out-Earn My Partner

Ouch. Maybe this one hasn't even crossed your mind. The sad reality in our times is that men earn more money than women. Period. But the happy reality is that women are taking the reins of their lives, opening businesses, and jumping into the driver's seat to propel themselves forward and earn more. And because of this, we may begin to see the tables turning.

When I worked as a licensed clinical social worker, I knew my income would be capped. I would have needed to work my buns off my entire life and hold roles with high responsibility in order to earn even half of what I am making now. Though it felt limiting, I am grateful for that situation because it gave me the motivation to create my own financial success. If I had remained an agency social worker, I would have needed to rely on a second income (my husband's) in order to take time off, go on vacations, and have even a little spending cash after my monthly student loan payment was deducted. (Please don't get me started on student loan debt and interest rates!) This is true for many women, and there is nothing wrong with it if it feels good for you. But I desired a little more leverage with how I could use my money.

Now ladies, even if you are creating your own income, there may be seasons when you need to rely on others for help financially, and there is nothing wrong with that! I have seen business friends borrow money from others in order to create a new product. I have seen clients borrow from family in order to meet the bills for a few months. And personally, I've been in seasons where my business was on hold (in order to mother) and have relied on my husband to pick up the weight of the household finances. So what I'm saying is that you don't need to out-earn others in order to feel successful—it's normal and okay to need help from time to time! But if you have dreams of increasing your earnings, go for it! If out-earning your partner is on the horizon, there should be no shame in it, only celebration for the success you're experiencing.

But if we find that we're afraid of out-earning our partner, where does this fear originate? First, throughout history men have often been the breadwinners while women took care of the household responsibilities. Maybe you watched your parents live out more traditional roles. Maybe you prefer traditional roles, and that is okay. But those who desire to earn more may need to determine whether they have a tendency to hold themselves back if it means they will surpass their partner's earnings.

If this is you, here are some questions to help unpack these feelings:

- What did your family roles look like growing up?
- Do you desire this same dynamic or something different?
- And for the single gals—what are your current views about future roles?
- If you're not out-earning your partner, how would you feel if you did? Do you have any personal objections around it?
- If you are in a relationship, have you had these conversations with your partner? If so, how did they go?

Most likely you are the one putting this limit on yourself, and your partner couldn't really care less (in a good way!) if you out-earn them. I hope this is the case for you. Yes, men are still out-earning women in the workforce, but I like to think we live in a day where the right men are in support of seeing their partners succeed beyond the limitations society has put on them. And if your partner is not happy for your success, I suggest you get some support from someone like a coach or therapist who can give you guidance with an unbiased opinion.

If I Succeed, I Will No Longer Be Humble

Am I the only one who is afraid that success equals a loss of humility? Keeping it real with you ladies that I still struggle with this fear big time. And let me clarify—just because I struggle with it doesn't mean that I allow it to hold me back! And you don't have to let it hold you back either. You can experience the thought or emotion but choose to continue moving forward in life. I often remind my clients that if they're worrying about whether they're humble, they're probably dealing with insecurity rather than pride. Remember, the more success you grab hold of, the bigger the magnifying glass will be that is held over you. If you are humble right where you are today as someone with one business, you will be just as humble when you've franchised your business and now have hundreds of locations.

I intentionally left this lie for last because there isn't much unpacking to do! I pretty much said it all—I believe in you and believe that if you, like me, struggle with this fear, most likely you *will* remain humble even in seasons of massive success. The key with remaining humble is staying grounded. The key with remaining grounded is experiencing empathy. And then, empathy will be your antidote to pride. It's crucial that as we find more success, we continually have little heart checks with ourselves to keep us grounded. And how can we do this? It's easy. Go back to a time when things weren't as abundant as today and feel some empathy for that past version of yourself. I bet getting to where you are today was not easy. You had to stretch and grow and make some sacrifices to reach the level of success you have today. And what this looks like for you today may simply be grabbing an old journal and flipping back through the pages, reading the entries from a time when you didn't have the things that you have today. This not only keeps you grounded by reminding you how fortunate you are today but also brings perspective if you're feeling success isn't happening fast enough. Because let's get real, ladies, we are all guilty of this! And if you aren't a paper-and-pen kind of girl, carve out a couple of minutes for mindful reflection of a time when things were different. I assure you that if you engage in these reflections every now and then, it will be much easier to remain grounded when success hits.

How to Succeed Like a Boss

Can you relate to the fears we've been talking about? Are you struggling with not feeling capable of handling #allthethings that success can bring? Maybe as you inch closer to your next big goal, you unknowingly stop yourself in fear of how relationships, your image, and your lifestyle will be impacted. You may even cling to roadblocks to unintentionally keep yourself safe. Each time this happens, you may not even notice you're sabotaging yourself and preventing the very things you want. You end up disappointed in yourself because you know that

205

your limiting beliefs are holding you back, and you feel like you'll never be able to move past this damaging behavior.

For some of you, reading about "fear of success" is an exhale moment. You've felt stuck on the same goals for months, maybe even years, and haven't quite been able to put a finger on why they still haven't come to fruition. As you've turned these pages, you've realized that because of some deep fears, you've remained where you're at because it's safe. While you value your dreams and the success you envision, the last thing you wanted was to lose friends, get lost in pride, wound your relationship, or fail to keep up with life in general. Now that we've addressed the top four scenarios that contribute to this lie, let's discuss two simple strategies to help overcome these limiting beliefs.

First of all, I want to teach you how to recognize self-sabotaging patterns before they even begin. Take a moment and think back to a situation when you feared success and started finding roadblocks to unintentionally hinder your path to success. When did this start, and how did it manifest? Did it start in your body? Maybe you noticed feeling a little more jittery. Maybe you caught yourself wanting to binge on Double Stuf Oreos and sleep all the time. Fear always begins internally and works its way out. After this, what were those next steps you took to self-sabotage? Did you tell yourself you were scared over and over again? Did you start avoiding your friends when they texted you? Did you stop sharing your business wins with others in fear they would judge you? Raising my hand over here. I've experienced each of these, and because I know what my patterns are, I can recognize these fears and speak the truth so they don't hold me back. Take a moment and jot down some of your self-sabotaging behaviors below. If you can't think of any, ask a friend!

Second, ask yourself this simple question: *What if I succeed? What am I really afraid will happen?* Is it possibly one of the four scenarios we touched on above, or is it something else? And whatever it is that you're afraid of, will you survive if it happens? I know I'm being sassy with you! Of course you will figure it out, continue to live, and—I believe—even thrive. Remember, the goal you so badly want to achieve can be possible for you if you can walk through the fear. Often the following steps are helpful to my clients when they're experiencing fear:

1. Remind yourself how badly you want to reach the desired outcome.
2. Envision what it will feel like to make it there.
3. Tell yourself, *I will survive no matter what—fear is just a feeling*.
4. Envisioning the success you desire and how it will *feel* to get there, review all limiting beliefs that are holding you back from moving forward.

Through all of this, remind yourself that you will figure it out when you get there. Instead of worrying about what will happen when you succeed, trust that you can handle it when you get there! Right? Ruminating on all of the what-ifs creates obstacles for actually getting to where you want to be. Repeat this after me: "I will worry about what could happen if I succeed when I succeed."

I know in the moment the fear of how you will handle a new season can be scary. But look, you've faced this before. You somehow worked through the fear to get to where you are today. Can you remind yourself you are capable of even more success in your future? Remember, you are only capable of achieving and handling whatever it is you believe you can handle. This is why it's so important that you recognize this limiting belief and remind yourself that you are smart and capable—you can handle new challenges and responsibilities, and as you step into new seasons, that's exactly what you'll do!

Conclusion:
THINKING LIKE A BOSS

As I was posing for the cover of this book, I paused for a moment to envision what you look like. Tears welled up thinking about the obstacles you have faced to get to where you are today. In that moment, I envisioned outstretching my arms and embracing you in a warm hug, reminding you that you are so much more powerful than you think.

Take a moment to applaud yourself. As I tell my clients all the time, mindset work is *not* for the faint of heart. It's one of the most difficult aspects of being a boss. It's much easier to immerse yourself in strategy, systems, and the processes of a business. Digging into your inner beliefs and mindsets takes work, and it sets the foundation for everything else that you do in life and in business. You can have all of the education and certifications in the world, but if your mindset isn't in check, you will be holding yourself back from your full potential. Mindset is what separates the winners from the forever learners. Right? Because in life we don't ever lose, we either win or we learn.[1] But your goal isn't to just continue learning lessons forever, it's to learn some lessons and win, learn some more and then win some more.

You are so much more capable than you can even fathom. There is no better time than now to begin living out of an abundance mindset, believing in your own capabilities and dreams. Remember, if an opportunity is presented to you and it's not a *heck yeah!* today, having more time next month will not make it a *heck yeah!* for you. More than anything, trust that inner voice—it won't let you down.

When all else fails, turn the screen off, step outside in nature, and get quiet. Pray, meditate, dream. Let your imagination run free. Those dreams that are within are yours to take hold of. They were placed on your heart because you are responsible enough to birth them. There are people waiting for what it is you have to give, and only *you* can tell your story and share your talents the way that you do. There is always enough to go around. Do not shrink back because someone else is already doing it. It is on your heart because your version of it is needed. Your fellow boss ladies need you, and you need them. Two are better than one, and there is strength in numbers. You are capable of making a much greater impact with four hands rather than two.

Every time you are experiencing any of these twelve lies, remember, it is because you are moving forward—you are growing and stepping into a new level of success rather than staying stagnant. I hope that you will keep this book somewhere handy so that when you begin to experience limiting mindsets, you can easily pick it up, flip to a chapter, and be reminded of your own capability to think like a boss.

Share these principles with others. Let's make them become a normal part of our everyday life. Let's not only champion ourselves and the women around us but also pave the way for the women behind us. Together we can build up our next generation of leaders and show them what is possible when you think—and live—like a boss. Love you, lady.

Acknowledgments

I'm not going to sugarcoat it; writing this book was harder than both pregnancies and childbirths combined. Putting these words on paper was one of the most mentally taxing things I have ever done, yet the most freeing and ultimately life-giving. Each chapter brought strenuous testing, which ultimately built up my capacity to handle even more. Talk about resiliency! First and foremost, none of this would be possible without Jesus. Thank you, Jesus, for giving me the strength to keep going when it would have been a lot easier to give up. Thank you for giving me a platform to share my story.

Andrew, this book would not exist if it weren't for you. You are my rock. You are the one person who believes in my big, crazy dreams. You never doubt my bold (and sometimes borderline delusional) ideas. You amaze me, juggling so many projects, and I am so proud of you for pursuing your own dreams and launching a restaurant during my last deadline. Teamwork makes the dream work.

Mom and Dad, thank you for all of the life lessons you've taught me—especially the lesson of living life with open hands, trusting there will always be enough. Thank you for always believing in me and never giving up during those teen years. Thank you for being prayer warriors even before I was born. And, last but not least, thank you for picking up the pieces when I needed to write!

Mama and Papa C, thank you for your constant championing, your emotional support, and your help with the babies to make this book happen. I knew *Thinking Like a Boss* had to be the title after you surprised me with that sign, Mama!

Em and Claud, thank you for helping with the girls. They adore their aunties!

Oma, thank you for your fine attention to detail, catching little typos in the early editing process. Thank you for the lessons you've passed along and for being our family prayer warrior!

Keely, you are a GEM—one in a million. Thank you for taking a chance on my story. Thank you for believing in me, even when I wasn't 100 percent sure that I yet believed in myself. Thank you for loving this book as much as I do and treating it as your own. Thank you, Wordserve Literary Agency, for welcoming me in.

Rachel, you and the entire Baker team have brought me on and treated me like family from the start. I am blown away with how you championed this book—from the very beginning you saw the vision and need to get this out into the world. The icing on the cake was brunch and Barnes and Noble book browsing in New York City with you and Rebekah. Such a perfect way to celebrate wrapping up the manuscript!

Patti, I love how fun you made the cover process. You have a gift for understanding the visual dream of your authors. The cover is even more fitting than I could have dreamed. Let's do a rain check for Dallas!

Meshali, your work is truly magical. Thank you for understanding our vision for the cover and capturing it perfectly with your camera. And you are a trouper, hopping on a plane, grabbing a rental car, and braving the New York traffic to make my shoot happen.

Alex, what a full-circle moment it was, having you do my makeup for my first-ever shoot three years ago and then for this book cover. I couldn't have been happier spending a day stranded in the airport with you and Charlie!

Rachel, Cassandra, and Jennie, thank you for all of your support in crafting and polishing my proposal.

Jenn, thank you for your style advice for the cover. Love the outfit you picked for me!

Kate and Sarah, thank you for the emotional support with our monthly Book Buddy calls. We are doing it, girls!

To all of my girlfriends, family members, clients, and tribe members who cheered me on throughout this whole process— I truly couldn't do this on my own. Your love notes and words of encouragement are what kept me going!

Notes

Introduction

1. Marsha Linehan, *Skills Training Manual for Treating Personality Disorder* (New York: Guilford, 1993).

Lie #1 I Need to Have It All Together

1. Amy Cuddy, "Your Body Language May Shape Who You Are," TED Talks, June 2012, accessed June 4, 2019, https://www.ted.com/talks/amy _cuddy_your_body_language_shapes_who_you_are?language=en.
2. Linehan, *Skills Training Manual*.

Lie #2 I'm Not Ready to Start

1. Linehan, *Skills Training Manual*.

Lie #3 I'm Not Qualified (I'm Not Smart Enough, Young Enough, or Old Enough to Succeed)

1. Linehan, *Skills Training Manual*, 230.

Lie #4 I Will Never Have Enough Money

1. Shelly Schwartz, "Most Americans, Rich or Not, Stressed about Money: Surveys," CNBC, August 3, 2015, https://www.cnbc.com/2015 /08/03/most-americans-rich-or-not-stressed-about-money-surveys .html.

2. Daymond John and Daniel Paisner, *The Power of Broke: How Empty Pockets, a Tight Budget, and a Hunger for Success Can Become Your Greatest Competitive Advantage* (New York: Random House, 2016).

3. Business Wire, "The Average U.S. Household Has Over 50 Unused Items Worth $3,100 According to eBay/Nielsen Survey," April 26, 2007, https://www.businesswire.com/news/home/20070426005614/en /Average-U.S.-Household-50-Unused-Items-Worth.

4. Irving Berlin, "Count Your Blessings (Instead of Sheep)," sung by Bing Crosby in the movie *White Christmas*, directed by Michael Curtiz (Hollywood, CA: Paramount Pictures, 1954).

5. Melody Beattie, *The Language of Letting Go* (Center City, MN: Hazeldon Publishing, 1990), 218.

Lie #5 Making Money Is Greedy

1. Kelly Lyndgaard, email message to author, May 21, 2019.

2. Cassandra Bodzak, "Episode 8: Cassandra Bodzak," interview by Kate Crocco, August 20, 2018, *Thinking Like a Boss*, podcast, https:// www.katecrocco.com/podcastblog/cassandrabodzak.

3. Brian and Bobbie Houston are the pastors and founders of Hillsong Church Sydney in Australia.

Lie #9 I Don't Have Enough Time

1. Google Dictionary, s.v. "boundary (*n.*)," accessed July 25, 2019, https://www.google.com/search?client=safari&rls=en&q=boundary &ie=UTF-8&oe=UTF-8.

Lie #10 It's Already Been Done Before

1. Marie Forleo, "5 Steal-Worthy Strategies from a Brand I Couldn't Resist," *Marie Forleo* (blog), January 2014, https://www.marieforleo.com /2014/01/stealworthy-branding-strategies/.

2. Jenn Sprinkle and Kelly Rucker, *Thirty-One Days of Prayer for the Dreamer and the Doer* (Fort Worth, TX: NyreePress, 2014).

Lie #12 I Am Not Capable of Handling Success

1. Gay Hendricks, *The Big Leap* (New York: HarperCollins, 2009).

Conclusion: Thinking Like a Boss

1. Author's paraphrase of a quote that is often attributed to Nelson Mandela.

Kate Crocco, MSW, LCSW, is a psychotherapist and a confidence and mindset coach who mentors female leaders around the globe. She has coached thousands of women through one-on-one, group, and mastermind programs, as well as through her Confident Ladies Club™ community. She is the host of a weekly podcast, *Thinking Like a Boss*, where she regularly interviews female entrepreneurs from various fields who have found success in business and in life. A guest expert on numerous podcasts and telesummits, Kate has been quoted in publications such as the *Huffington Post*, *Best Kept Self*, *SheKnows*, and *BlogHer*. Kate's mission is to lovingly challenge women to step into the best version of themselves and to empower them to go after their dreams by helping to break down the walls and fears that have been holding them back from greatness. Kate currently resides in New York with her husband, her two sweet girls, and her rescue pup, Turbo.

Connect with Kate

KATECROCCO.COM/PODCAST

Join
THE CONFIDENT LADIES CLUB
FACEBOOK COMMUNITY

THE CONFIDENT LADIES CLUB
with Kate Crocco

@katecrocco   Thinking Like A Boss Podcast

Be part of a community of *supportive, heart-centered, miracle-working* lady bosses.

CLAIM YOUR **FREE**
Success Kit

Sign up now for your
Confident Ladies Success Kit and you'll get:

- THE MINDSET RESET WORKBOOK: Hit the reset button on your mindset and reprogram it for success.
- THE BUILDING CONFIDENCE WORKBOOK: Overcome the "imposter syndrome" so you can build your confidence.
- THE VISIBILITY WORKBOOK: The exact steps Kate took to go from no business to a full and thriving coaching practice within 90 days.

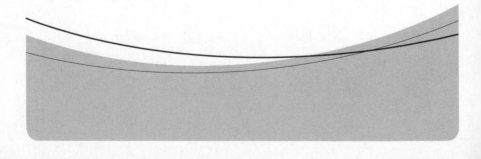